(handwritten inscription)

TREASURES

OF THE CHURCH

THAT WHICH MAKES US CATHOLIC

(handwritten inscription and signature)

Journeys of Faith®

1-800-633-2484

Bob & Penny Lord

Other Books by Bob and Penny Lord

THIS IS MY BODY, THIS IS MY BLOOD
Miracles of the Eucharist - Book I
THIS IS MY BODY, THIS IS MY BLOOD
Miracles of the Eucharist - Book II
THE MANY FACES OF MARY
a Love Story
WE CAME BACK TO JESUS
SAINTS AND OTHER POWERFUL WOMEN
IN THE CHURCH
SAINTS AND OTHER POWERFUL MEN
IN THE CHURCH
HEAVENLY ARMY OF ANGELS
SCANDAL OF THE CROSS AND ITS TRIUMPH
MARTYRS - THEY DIED FOR CHRIST
THE ROSARY - THE LIFE OF JESUS AND MARY
VISIONARIES, MYSTICS AND STIGMATISTS
VISIONS OF HEAVEN, HELL & PURGATORY
ESTE ES MI CUERPO, ESTA ES MI SANGRE
Milagros de la Eucaristía
LOS MUCHOS ROSTROS DE MARIA
una historia de amor

Table of Contents

Dedication

Pope John Paul II

His Holiness represents Church to us. While we did not sit down and collaborate on these books with him personally, all the material we used came to us as a result of his tenure as Pontiff of the Holy Roman Catholic Church. *Thank you, your Holiness, for keeping us going.*

Mother Angelica
and her **Poor Clare Nuns of Perpetual Adoration**

Mother Angelica, with her solemn vow to save the Church, has been a source of strength for us, since we began our Ministry, *encouraging* us with her unconditional commitment to bring Jesus to the world, *inflaming* us with her relentless dedication, *spurring* us on with her never waning stamina to be more, *inspiring* us to not look at the cost, *propelling* us to fight the good fight!

She has believed in us; we believe in her. *"We love you Mother Angelica, for who you are, but more for what you do for our Church."* That probably sums up who Mother is for us. *Thank you, Mother for giving us the courage to go on.*

As always, when in need of prayers and help, there is an army of faithful *Brides of Christ* ever ready to say Yes! Thank you for the example you have set for us and our Ministry, of faithfulness to your vocations. We would like to thank you and the Missionaries of the Eternal Word for all the information provided for our research, in getting us material which is impossible to find. We know there must be at least 483 Angels helping out there full time. *We thank you for your prayers, for your love, and for your help.*

Ted and Beverly Miller

Our Louisiana contingency, we call Beverly Ann and Ted the *Miller Media Research Company*, they have been sending books, faxing articles and e-mailing whatever they think we'll need to get the job done. They have been supporters for twelve years. *We thank y'all.*

Brother Joseph and Luz Elena

They have always deserved credit. They have always been there to make things work, Brother Joseph for almost ten years, and Luz Elena for thirteen. They have always been our support system, sharing our joys and our sorrows, our support in good times and bad. However this year they have taken on an almost impossible task. They insisted we go home to work on these three books while they run *everything* at the office. And they have done an outstanding job; they have given us much hope for the future of our ministry and our Church. *Thank you Brother Joseph and Luz Elena for always being there.*

Our most beloved family - our grandchildren

Rob and Andrea Ziminsky

If you need proof that God hears prayers, just come and meet our two grandchildren. Thirty years ago, God sent us Rob, the most wonderful grandson the world has ever known, outside of Jesus. We thought our cup runneth over, and then in His most generous, loving Sacred Heart Jesus sent us Andrea, Rob's wife - our precious granddaughter. They have made us so proud with their tireless devotion to the Church, working with the Youth!

The Volunteers and employees at Journeys of Faith

We want to thank all of you, for all your help throughout the years, those in California, those in Louisiana and all over the world. We thank you; we know that Jesus and Mary love and thank you. You are the Angels who have believed in us and in the work we do, and you have backed up that belief with your prayers and financial and physical help. *We ask all God's blessings on you.*

For anyone out there whom we have missed, and there are many, please forgive us; God bless you. We love you!

"Hell will not prevail against My Church"

My brothers and sisters, it seems like we begin every one of our books with a cry of urgency to Catholics the world over to unite and rally around our Pope and the Magisterium[1] of the Church. Having done the vast amount of research that was necessary to bring you the three books of this Trilogy on our Church, we know these are *not* the worst of times. These are not great times, but we, as a people of God under attack by the enemy, have been through worse. We have survived. Jesus' promise has always been good, "*I will be with you always, until the end of the world.*" and "*The gates of Hell will not prevail against my Church.*"

You may ask yourselves, in view of that statement, why does it seem like we are losing the battle. We are experiencing a crisis in our Church. The enemy is attacking on all sides, within and without the Church. Those who would destroy us are multi-faceted; they invade so quickly from so many directions we don't know where to turn and how to fight. They don't rest. When we, the people of God think we've won a particular battle, we tend to sit back and take a breather, rest on our laurels. But the enemy *never rests!* While we're fighting on one battlefield, great advances are being heaped up against us on other battlegrounds. We find ourselves and our Church constantly on the defensive.

---

[1]The Church's teaching authority, instituted by Christ and guided by the Holy Spirit, which seeks to safeguard and explain the Truths of the faith. The Magisterium is exercised in two ways: 1)Extraordinary, when the Pope and ecumenical councils infallibly define a Truth of faith or morals...2)Ordinary, when the Church infallibly defines Truths of the Faith (a)taught universally and without dissent (b)which must be taught or the Magisterium would be failing in its duty, (c)connected with a grave matter of faith or morals, and (d) which is taught authoritatively. (resource Catholic Encyclopedia, OSV)

But there is another side of the coin. Mother Church is so rich, so full, so exciting. Our Lord Jesus loves us so much, He has given us an abundance of *Treasures* to fight off the enemy, to help us journey through our Pilgrimage of life, to give us strength to stand up against the fires of hell. We can just envision the urgency of Jesus, as He went through the three years of His public ministry, teaching the people, teaching the Apostles, rushing to be sure He left us everything we would need to ward off the attacks He knew would be forthcoming, accelerating as we came closer to the end of the race here on earth. Picture Him high on the mountain, sharing a *How to live our Faith* Beatitudes - *"Blessed are the poor in spirit...."* Then run with Him to Capharnaum where He gives the discourse on the Bread of Life, the powerful mandate of John 6:51. *"I myself am the living Bread come down from Heaven. If anyone eats this Bread, he will live forever, and the Bread that I give is My Flesh, for the life of the world."*

As the Triumph of the Cross came nearer, He worked harder and harder to give us what He knew we would need. He brought all His trusted Apostles together at the Last Supper to complete the mandate; He gave us His Body and Blood in the Eucharist, keeping His promise that He would always be with us. He gave us the Priesthood at the Last Supper.

While Our Lord Jesus hung on the Cross, struggling to breathe, putting Himself through excruciating pain by lifting His Body with His Legs, in agony from the spikes which had been pounded through His Feet, opening up His rib cage in order to gather enough breath to utter a few last words to us, He gave us His Mother to be our Mother and the Mother of the Church at the foot of the Cross. He was that thorough giving us these gifts, these Treasures which make up the bouquet of flowers in the garden of the Church. Jesus left nothing to chance. He knew what we would be up against from the evil one and his cohorts when He was no longer with us. No sooner did He ascend to Heaven than the onslaught began fast and furiously.

From the very beginning, Satan has forced us to go on the offensive. We have found, as we've researched the history of our Church and the various Councils which have been called, that we don't really defend a Truth and define it until it's been attacked pretty violently. These are Truths in which we have always believed. But the enemy has played right into the hands of Jesus; he has forced us to define Truths which have become for us the **Treasures of our Church.** These Treasures form the Deposit of Faith, the Magisterium, that rock on which we stand as Catholics. These gifts were given to us directly by Our Lord Jesus while He walked the earth. They give us the endurance, the solid footing we need to fight the enemy who would throw us off the Rock of our Church and have us dash our souls against the craggy depths descending into the pits of Hell.

Our Lord Jesus gave us these tools, weapons if you will, to unite us as a People of God and Soldiers of Christ's Church on earth.

Jesus prayed to the Father for unity among His people:
"I do not pray for them alone.
I pray also for those who will believe in Me
through their word,
that all may be one
as You, Father, are in Me, And I in You;
I pray that they may be (one) in Us,
that the world may believe that You sent me.
I have given them the glory You gave Me
that they may be one, as We are one -
I living in them, You living in Me -
that their unity may be complete.
So shall the world know that You sent Me,

and that You loved them as You loved Me."[2]

Jesus commanded the Disciples to tell *all* the brothers and sisters that *in order for the world to believe that His Father sent Him*, they must be *united* not only with Him and His Father *but with one another*. Lord, forgive us; we've allowed the enemy to head us in just the opposite direction. Rather than being united, we become more fragmented than we've ever been in our history. Rather than telling the world to believe that His Father sent Him, the enemy began planting his poison immediately, putting doubt in the minds of the faithful that the Father sent Jesus at all.

From the very beginning, Satan's methods of attack have been to denounce, malign, slander and take away these most important Treasures of our Church. If Jesus believed they were important enough to leave them to us, you have to know that the evil one *knows* they're important enough to discredit and destroy.

The greatest attacks the enemy uses to discredit our firm beliefs and separate us from our Christian brothers and sisters is a pat phrase which is so incorrect, *"It's not in the Bible. Where can you find it in the Bible?"* And we Catholics panic because we don't really know the Bible. If we did know the Bible, we would realize that all the Truths of our Church are Scripture-based. Why do you think there has been such a rash of conversions of hard-line Protestant ministers to the Catholic Church? They proclaim that of all the denominations in the Church, the Catholic Church is the most Scripture-based of all. But in addition to Scripture, which came after the life-experience, we base our Faith Belief heavily on Tradition and the working of the Holy Spirit down through the centuries.

In this, the first book of the Trilogy, we want to share with you beliefs of the Catholic Faith which make up the

---

[2]Jn 17:20-23

Deposit of Faith, but are not accepted by our separated brothers and sisters in Christ. We want to give you all the background we have on these Truths, the Scripture Base, Catechism of the Catholic Church references as well as the Catholic Encyclopedia, teaching of the Saints - in particular, our Doctors of the Church - Saints who have passed the test of time and whose writings are used in the teachings of our Church.

You need to know these Truths when a member of a Protestant persuasion challenges our Faith or a cult member knocks on your door and tells you that Catholics do not teach according to the Bible. You have to know how you can defend yourself and your Church. You must know that most cults don't believe in the Bible entirely. Some twist it to their own advantage. Some add to it, to change it; others will only accept parts of it. Many don't accept the Old Testament. Others use the Bible to get you to listen to them and then berate the Truths of our Church.

You also must know if someone in our own Church preaches heresy regarding the Truths of our Church, or downright denies Truths of our Church, what is correct, and where it came from. This is a time of battle. We must defend our Church against all who would destroy it in any way.

In Book II, we will give you a background of the Tragedy of the Protestant Reformation, how it came about, and how it has affected our Church. In Book III, we want to tell you about the most popular but deadly influence on Catholics today, the cults and non-denominational religions. We will give you their background, and what they are doing to turn Catholics around to their way of believing.

It's important, my brothers and sisters, that you learn these Treasures and take them to heart. Our Church is in danger; you are the ones the Lord wants to use to prevent the gates of hell from prevailing against His Church and destroying it.

Jesus made a promise, "*The gates of Hell will not prevail against it (His Church).*" You and I are the means He uses to keep that promise. Come with us now on this Journey of Faith. When we are finished, we pray you will have been given strength and discernment which can only come from Our Lord Jesus through His Holy Spirit. We pray you will don the armor St. Paul speaks of. The war is real; the enemy is real. We need you; Jesus needs you. Our Church cannot survive without you. Praise God in all things.

Pope John Paul II
Vicar of Christ
on Earth

Above: ***Pope John Paul II is the living successor of St. Peter***

Above: ***Bob and Penny Lord at an audience with our beloved
Pope John Paul II - an unforgettable experience.***

Thou art Peter....

"Thou art Peter, and upon this Rock I will build My Church."[1]

Our chapter opens with Our Lord and His raggedy band of twelve making their last journey together. One would betray Him, one would deny Him, and all would desert Him except for a teen-age boy, John the Beloved.

They followed Him to *Caesarea Philippi*,[2] where He had preached on the Kingdom, the Reign of God. Caesarea Philippi was destined to be a place of major significance for time immemorial, because it was here that Our Lord Jesus created the Church; here He commissioned Peter as its head, and our first Pope. Here, He prepared the Apostles for their roles in the New Church.

It was evening. They had finished their meal by a fireplace. The day had been exciting; believers were added by the droves; the Word of God had been extolled; healings had taken place; people hung on His every word.

Jesus asked the Apostles what the reactions of the people were that day. What were they saying? Who did they say He was? The Apostles gave various reports. Some said He was John the Baptist, others Moses or one of the prophets. He pressed on, *"But who do you say that I am?"* Simon Peter, filled with the Holy Spirit, rose and cried out, *"You are the Christ, the Son of the living God!"*[3]

A great silence overtook them. This was the moment Jesus had been waiting for. He looked deeply into Peter's eyes and proclaimed:

*"Blessed art **thou**, Simon Bar-Jona; because flesh and blood hath not revealed it to **thee**, but My Father who is in Heaven. And I say to **thee**: That **thou** art Peter, and upon this rock I will build My Church, and the jaws of*

---

[1] Mt 16:18
[2] in the northeastern section of Palestine
[3] Mt 16:16-18

13

*Hell shall not prevail against it. And I will give to **thee**
the keys of the Kingdom of Heaven. And whatsoever
thou shalt bind upon earth, it shall be bound in Heaven;
and whatsoever **thou** shalt loose on earth shall be
loosed also in Heaven."*[4]

He chose Peter, he to whom the Father had revealed
His Son. And when that came to pass, the gates of Heaven
swung wide open; the Angels in Heaven, the Cherubim and
Seraphim, all nine choirs proclaimed praises of Alleluia to
the glory of God; the warm glow of the Father streamed
down from Heaven, surrounding, enveloping and caressing
Jesus and His modest little band of followers at Caesarea
Philippi; the wind of the Holy Spirit filled them with courage,
determination, tenacity and boldness. This was the moment
the world had waited for. This was truly the beginning.

Some days later, in Matthew's Gospel when Jesus was
teaching, He spoke to the rest of the Apostles and disciples,
*"Amen I say to **you**, whatsoever **you** shall bind upon earth, shall
be bound also in Heaven; and whatsoever **you** shall loose upon
earth, shall be loosed also in Heaven."*[5]

✝✝✝

It's important to recognize the *difference* between the
use of *thee* and *you*. We've highlighted the *thee's* and *thou's*
in Jesus' discourse to Peter, to show how Jesus used them
solely when He spoke to Peter. This He did, as Jesus was
solely directing *Peter* to be head of the Church. Jesus
referred to Peter seven times in this passage, using the
pronouns for Peter, *"thee* and *thou."*[6]

Jesus didn't say to the rest of the Apostles and disciples,
"I say to *thee*" but "I say to *you*."[7] So when Jesus spoke to

---

[4]Mt 16:18-20 We're using the Douay-Rheims version of the Holy
Bible here to emphasize the Lord's use of thee and thou for Peter.

[5]Mt 18:18 from the Douay-Rheims Catholic version of the Bible.

[6]Mt 16:18-20

[7]Mt 18:18

Peter,[8] He very carefully zeroed in on *Peter personally*, giving him the special mandate to be the head of the Church. When He spoke to the Apostles and disciples a few days later,[9] He was speaking to all of them *collectively*, therefore He spoke in the plural, or *you*. To recap, four promises were made to Peter *individually*, Jesus using *thee* and *thou* when speaking *solely* to Peter: (1)"*And I say to thee: that thou art Peter and upon this rock I will build My Church.*" (2) "*The gates of hell shall not prevail against it.*" (3) "*And I will give thee the keys of the kingdom of heaven.*" and (4) "*And whatsoever thou shalt bind upon earth, it shall be bound also in heaven; and whatsoever thou shalt loose on earth, it shall be loosed in heaven.*"

Then later, granting the fourth promise to all the Apostles, Jesus does not use the singular *thou* that He used for Peter, He uses the plural *you* to speak to them *collectively*, "*Amen I say to you, whatsoever you shall bind upon earth, shall be bound also in heaven, and whatsoever you shall loose upon earth, shall be loosed in heaven.*" This in no way lessened the powers of Peter, or his place as the head of the Church. It was clearly understood by all that their powers were to be used under the leadership of Peter. "*His powers included theirs; theirs did not include his.*"[10]

We always thought that the Mandate given by Our Lord Jesus to Peter and the Apostles, *to bind and loose*, was exclusively the power to forgive or not forgive sins. However, it goes far beyond that. Jesus, being of the Jewish people,[11] when He used the terms *bind and loose*, He was

---

[8]Mt 16:16-18

[9]Mt 18:18

[10]from Catholics, Protestants, and the Bible - Pauline Singleman

[11]Jesus knew and understood the Law of His ancestors- the rabbinical law. And remember, He said "*I have not come to do away with the Law...*"

declaring that He was giving them the *authority* to *bind and loose*, to teach and discipline.

We go to the meaning that these words had for the Jews, the rabbis who were given these powers. The power to bind and loose, which were given to Peter and the Apostles and their successors mean the following:

Bind: To teach - *To declare authoritatively that some thing is obligatory.*

To discipline - *The power to pronounce the sentence of excommunication upon an individual or of interdict[12] upon a community.*

Loose: To teach - *Declare authoritatively that there is no moral obligation.*

To discipline - *The power to revoke a sentence of excommunication or interdict.*

So these two powers to bind and loose, not only gave our Pope, Apostles and those who followed, the powers to forgive sins, to teach and discipline, it gave them the authority with the Pope, the Head of the Church, as the supreme authority.

Often it's important to have a Douay-Rheims Bible, so that you can see the translations from the Bible in language which is more explicit than is possible in modern English. In this instance, it's crucial. In the King James version of the Bible, which is the official Protestant standard, old English is used; the Scripture passages are the same, but Protestant commentaries don't mention the difference between the pronouns *thee* and *you*, or the great significance this has on the meaning of Scripture, how it affects especially these particular passages.[13] This section where Jesus calls Peter *Rock* is one of the most powerful and also one of the most controversial Scripture passages in the Bible. For Catholics,

---

[12]to exclude (a parish, person, etc) from certain acts, Sacraments or privileges

[13]Mt 16:16-18

it represents Peter the Rock upon which Jesus built *His* Church, Jesus' own proclamation of His Church and Peter as Head of His Church. It also gave Peter and his successors the power to teach and discipline. *Protestants disagree with us violently on this point.* They refuse to accept the Primacy of Peter and will do anything they can to discredit this passage.

†††

After having given these mandates at Caesarea, Jesus chose *Peter*, James and John to go up with Him to Mount Tabor, a mountaintop where Jesus would grant them the gift of seeing Him *transfigured* into His Divine State. Upon seeing their Lord radiant, a white aura encompassing Him, they exclaimed "*Lord how good it is for us to be here!*" Only three were with Jesus! He chose three: *Peter* who would lead His Church after He ascends to Heaven, *James* who would stress the need of putting our Christianity to work and *John* who would go with Him to the Cross. [In Holy Scripture, it is *Peter* we see involved with Jesus at key times in His ministry; it is Peter we hear speaking for the other Apostles; it is always Peter the first mentioned in Holy Scripture, preceding the other Apostles.]

Jesus brought these specially chosen three because they would need strength for what was ahead - the Lord's last journey: His Passion and death on the Cross on another hilltop, Calvary. They would need courage and dedication to embark, without their Savior, on their great journey as Evangelists, twelve completely unequipped preachers, who would bring the name of Jesus to the whole world. But Jesus knew they would need a leader to guide them, and that is why, one of His last acts, before His ascent to Calvary and the Cross, was to give them and us a leader on earth, our Pope. *Long may he live!*

Jesus knew that a family needs a father. He had an earthly father, His foster father St. Joseph. Although Jesus' Heavenly Father is, was and always will be omnipotent, King of Kings, He sent Jesus an earthly father to whom He would pledge obedience! Jesus, Who was God-man, obeyed an earthly Mother and foster father. God had entrusted a mortal, St. Joseph, with the awesome gift and overwhelming responsibility to care for, guide and protect His Holy Family!

Loving us, God, through the wisdom of the Second Person of the Holy Trinity, our Jesus, passed on this foster fatherhood to the first Pope, St. Peter, and to all 261 Popes who followed him, who have sat and now sit in the chair of Peter. Obedience to this foster father whom Jesus gave us, our Pope, binds us together, unites us in response to Jesus' prayer at the Last Supper *"that they may all be one; even as Thou, Father, art in Me, and I in Thee, that they also may be in Us."*[14]

We know what we believe and we speak what we believe. This is our Catholic Faith; this is what we believe in. These are our Treasures. God our Father so loves us, He sent His only begotten Son to save us from the fires of Hell, to put out the fires fueled by the sin of our original parents, Adam and Eve, and through His suffering to open the gates of Heaven for us.

Yet, this is one of the forms of obedience that separate us from our Protestant brothers and sisters in Christ. How could this be? Jesus knew His time was short; He told his Apostles He was to suffer and die; how important was it, that Jesus took the precious time He had left, to choose Peter as the Rock upon which He would build His Church! One of Jesus' most compassionate acts, before He went to the Father, was leaving His Church and all its Faculties to the Apostles under the headship of St. Peter, so that we His sheep would not be without a shepherd. Nevertheless, the Pope was one of the first of our sacred Treasures attacked by Martin Luther, Calvin and Henry VIII.

---

[14]Jn 17:21

Our Popes, our successors of Peter, our Vicars, *our Sweet Christs on Earth,*[15] had their beginnings in very humble but passionate circumstances. There was no great fanfare. There were no great ceremonies. There was first Caesaria and Jesus' commissioning of Peter; there was the undying love of Jesus, His powerful voice and urgency eager to put things in order before He left; there was that moment on the Cross when the Church flowed from Jesus' Pierced Heart; there was the power breathed into the Apostles through the wind of the Holy Spirit.[16] There was (and is) Jesus alive, talking through His Vicar on earth, the Pope.

This book is not meant to criticize brothers and sisters in Christ, or for that matter, any cults or sects which do not agree with our Faith. But we as Catholics must know what they believe in or don't believe in. Have you ever wondered why Fundamentalists, those who claim complete faith in the Bible, reject important Truths that we believe in which are backed up by Scripture? A main source of contention, just *one* of many instances where they don't interpret the Bible as we who originated the Bible do, and have done for 2000 years, is the Scripture Passage where Jesus declares the Primacy of Peter. This is an example of what can be found in some Protestant Biblical Commentaries about Matthew 16:17-19 regarding the Primacy of Peter:

> "This paragraph has presented unusual difficulties to scholars and widely divergent views are held both concerning its genuineness and its real meaning. *I regard it as a later addition inserted by the Evangelist* to give sanction to the claim of priority made for Peter by the early Church..."[17]

Whoa! So some Protestants can write off this passage, upon which we Catholics have built our Church, as *a plot* by

---

[15]Loving term coined for the Pope by St. Catherine of Siena
[16]Jn 3:8
[17]Abingdon Commentary, Abingdon Press, 1929, #980

the authors of the Gospel to manipulate Scripture for the
purpose of affirming the Primacy of Peter. What they're
saying here in fact, is that the Bible cannot be totally
accepted as Truth because in certain instances, (*which go
against their own beliefs*) the Gospel writers misrepresented
the actual events to conform to their own agenda. That is a
terrible accusation to make which cannot be proven or
disproved, as well as most of the Bible. It not only attacks
the Catholic Church, it contradicts everything the many
Protestant denominations preach, as they hold the Bible the
sole basis for their belief. If that passage is not true, is
anything true? They just took our Savior from us, along with
God the Father.

Another area of contention regarding this Scripture
passage which gave us our Church and Peter as its head, is
the Greek translation of the word *Rock*. The Greeks have
two words for rock. They used *Petro*s for Peter, which is
masculine, and *Petra* for the Church, which is feminine.
Therefore, "Thou art Peter (Petros) and upon this rock
(petra) I will build my Church."[18] The Greek interpreter
mistakenly used *petra*, the feminine because the Church is
feminine in Greek;[19] but Jesus was not saying upon this
Church, I will build My Church; He was saying upon this
Rock (referring to Peter, masculine), I will build My Church.
But sadly, the enemy has used this to divide and destroy the
New Jerusalem,[20] down through the centuries. The most
tragic, and ironic part of it all is that Aramaic, which is the
language Jesus spoke, *does not have* two words for rock.
They have **Kephas**, which means Rock and that's it. So when

---

[18]A case could be made that the translator used the feminine for
rock meaning Church because Church is a feminine word. We call her
Mother Church. But it was not a good liberty to take with such a crucial
passage.

[19]and most latin based languages as well

[20]the Roman Catholic Church

it was written, "*Thou art rock, and upon this rock.....*" it meant just one thing, *Rock.*

And yet, those who will not accept the Primacy of Peter manipulate that into meaning that Peter was not a rock, but a small stone.   In fact, a wounding commentary on this passage reads:

"How little Peter understood (Matthew 16:18)[21] *is evident from* (Matthew 16:22, 23)[22] *[Here they refer to Peter's impetuous expression of affection.] He who had just been called **a rock to build on is now a stone to stumble over!**"[23]*

A recent convert from Protestantism to the Catholic Church, James Akin, in an excellent book called *Surprised by Truth,*[24] summed up how ridiculous this whole hypothesis is. He interpreted the above Scripture Passage according to what the Protestant commentaries would have us believe was said.   Jesus said to Peter: "*Blessed are you, Simon Bar-Jonah. You are an **insignificant** little pebble.   Here are the keys to the kingdom of Heaven.*"

I would like to take a moment here, to be offended, not only for Catholics of today but for those who came before, ancestors of the very Protestants who are casting these unworthy stones at the Father Apostle of our Church, St. Peter.   In an attempt to advance their own agenda, and in order to accomplish their own ends, we wonder how far they are willing to go, these followers of Luther who appear hell-bent on discrediting St. Peter, criticizing and ridiculing him, as they willfully deny him his rightful place as the head of our Church - a title given him by Our Lord Jesus.   After all, he

---

[21]that he is Rock
[22]when Peter pleads: "*God forbid, Lord.   No such thing shall ever happen to you.*"
[23] Abingdon 981 from *Catholics, Protestants and the Bible*
[24]Published by Basilica Press - PO Box 85152-134 San Diego, CA 92186

was the *Prince of the Apostles*, the right hand man of Jesus. No matter what you want to believe about his role in the Church, you cannot deny how close to Jesus he was. In the Acts of the Apostles, after the death of Jesus, any time the Apostles are mentioned, Peter is the first name, because of his position. Doesn't that account for something, for a little respect? He left family and home; he gave up everything for Jesus and the Gospel. He was a martyr for our faith. Is all that of no account?

These people who were and continue to be so willing to sacrifice Peter for their own gains are casting mud on a major Saint. They're spreading slander against a prince of the Church. And it's not just our Church; it's their Church, too. Or at least it was. And to be very honest, to use that kind of character assassination doesn't put the maligners in a very good light. Where is Jesus in that?

Feed My Lambs....Feed My Sheep

Another major affirmation of the role given to Peter by our Lord Jesus appears at the end of St. John's gospel:

Jesus appeared to the Apostles on the Sea of Galilee. *"When they had eaten their meal, Jesus said to Simon Peter, 'Simon, son of John, do you love Me more than these?' 'Yes, Lord,' Peter said, 'You know that I love You.' At which Jesus said 'Feed My Lambs.' A second time He put His question, 'Simon, son of John, do you love Me?' 'Yes, Lord,' Peter said, 'You know that I love You.' Jesus replied, 'Tend My Sheep.' A third time Jesus asked him, 'Simon, son of John, do you love Me?' Peter was hurt because He had asked a third time, 'Do you love Me?' So he said to Him: 'Lord, You know everything. You know well that I love You.' Jesus said to Him, 'Feed My Sheep.'"*[25]

---

[25] Jn 21:15-17

This is a powerful confirmation of Peter's role and position in the Church. Jesus did not ask any of the others to feed His sheep, only the man He had made the shepherd, Peter. This Scripture passage represents the fulfillment by Jesus of the promise made to Peter in Matthew 16:18-20.

The New Catholic Encyclopedia makes a very important point about these two passages with regard to the Papacy:

"Both passages gave rise to the claim of two kinds of primacy in the Roman Church: a *magisterial* and a *jurisdictional* primacy. The former[26] is concerned with the final definition of the doctrine and teaching; the latter[27] with government in the sense of a final decision."

The Catholic Encyclopedia goes on to say:

"The essential point, which was invariably stressed by the Papacy, was that in the Biblical passages, notably in the Matthean (Matthew) verses, *Christ founded a new society, namely the Church,* and *provided a government* for the Church by conferring on Peter a *fullness of power.* It was a unique, creative act of Christ Himself.

"Further, since the Church was never, from the papal point of view, a merely spiritual or sacramental body, but an organized, visible, juristic and corporate society that needed constant guidance for the realization of its aims, the conferment of governmental powers on Peter implicitly and necessarily contained the provision for a succession into these powers, specifically bestowed as they were on the Prince of the Apostles."[28]

Infallibility

As with most dogmas of the Church, the doctrine of *Infallibility* has been believed and accepted from the

---

[26]Mt 16:18-19
[27]Jn 21:17
[28]New Catholic Encyclopedia Volume 10, Page 951

beginning of the Church. However in the middle of the nineteenth century, the Church and the world were in the throws of Pantheism[29] and the Age of Reason, where all things *supernatural* were being questioned and ultimately denied. In addition, there were historians and theologians who were trying to diminish the authority of the Church in theological matters. It was time for *Infallibility* to be proclaimed as a dogma of the Church. For this purpose, Vatican Council I was held. The doctrine, *Paeter aeternus* defined the jurisdictional primacy and the infallibility of the Pope on July 18, 1870.

Jesus affirms Infallibility in the following Scripture:

*"I no longer speak of you as slaves, for a slave does not know what his Master is about. Instead, I call you friends, **since I have made known to you all that I heard from My Father.**"*[30]

*"When He comes (the Paraclete), however, being the Spirit of Truth, He will guide you to all truth. **He will not speak on His own, but will speak only what He hears and will announce to you the things to come.** "*[31]

*"Simon, Simon! Remember that Satan has asked for you, to sift you all like wheat. **But I have prayed for you that your Faith may never fail.** You in turn must strengthen your brothers."*[32]

Then St. Paul speaks of it in Galatians 1:9:

"I repeat what I have just said: if anyone preaches a Gospel to you other than the one you received, let a curse be upon him."

And then again in Ephesians 4:11-13:

"It is He (Jesus) who gave Apostles, Prophets, Evangelists, Pastors and Teachers in roles of service for the Faithful to build up the body of Christ, till we become one in Faith and in the

---

[29]Pope Pius IX condemned Pantheism in 1861
[30]Jn 15:15
[31]Jn 16:13
[32]Lk 22:31-32

knowledge of God's Son, and form that perfect man who is Christ come to full stature."

St. Ireneaus, an early Church Father, called the Church the *"Charisma of Truth"*. And there are so many references, it would fill a book.

The *Doctrine of Infallibility* defines infallibility as being:

(1) in the Pope personally and solely as the successor of St. Peter,

(2) in an Ecumenical Council *subject to confirmation* by the Pope,

(3) in the bishops of the Universal Church teaching *definitively in union* with the Pope.

As such, "Infallibility does not extend to pronouncements on discipline and Church policy and by no means includes impeccability of the Pope or inerrancy in his private opinions. It is, briefly, the assured guarantee of the unfolding of the Apostolic Deposit of Faith by authority of the Church whereby Christ's doctrine must and will be handed on by an infallible Church guided by the Holy Spirit."[33]

The Primacy of Peter and his successors has never been a *new invention* of the Catholic Church. At the opening of the Council of Ephesus in 431 AD, Philip, a priest and papal legate, addressed the assembled bishops with these words:

"No one doubts, in fact, it is obvious to all ages that the holy and most Blessed Peter, head and Prince of the Apostles, the pillar of faith, and the foundation of the Catholic Church, received the keys of the kingdom from our Lord Jesus Christ, the Savior and the Redeemer of the human race. Nor does anyone doubt that the power of forgiving and retaining sins was also given to this same Peter who, in his successors, lives and exercises judgment even to this time and forever."

---

[33]Catholic Encyclopedia - Broderick

This same paragraph was repeated in the Dogmatic Constitution of the Church, Chapter 2, "*The Continuation of St. Peter's Primacy in the Roman Pontiffs*" on July 18, 1870 at Vatican Council I.

Finally, we will quote from the beginning of Chapter One of that document, "*The Establishment of the Apostolic Primacy in St. Peter*":

"We teach and declare, therefore, according to the testimony of the Gospel that the primacy of jurisdiction over the whole Church of God was immediately and directly promised to and conferred upon the blessed Apostle Peter by Christ the Lord."

The Papacy, as handed down to us by Jesus Himself, is very important to us Catholics. We believe our Popes are successors of St. Peter. We back that belief up with volumes of documentation. We don't require that anyone else believe it, but this is our Faith; this is who we are, and we demand respect for what we believe in. We have had good Popes and not so good Popes. And yet the Lord has protected His Church in spite of these problems. Our current Pope, Pope John Paul II, has been one of the most powerful forces in the Church and in the world. We revere him greatly as being one of the strongest successors to St. Peter the Church has ever had.

It's important that you, our Catholic brothers and sisters, understand what we, as Catholics believe, and where it came from. As you can see, all of our teachings about the Pope and the Infallibility of the Pope are Scripture Based. You must know who we are if you're going to defend our Faith and evangelize to those who do not. Learn all you can. *Your Church needs you!*

The Holy Trinity

Central Mystery of Christian Faith and Life

"In the Name of the Father and of the Son and of the Holy Spirit." We say it, but do we know what we're saying; are we really aware of the awesome truth we're proclaiming? Many of our newer, more traditional priests, before they begin to pray the Mass, preface it with, *"As we should begin all things, let us begin in the Name of the Father and of the Son and of the Holy Spirit."*

What are we doing when we make the Sign of the Cross? We are proclaiming our belief in the Most Holy Trinity, *the greatest of the revealed mysteries of Christianity."*[1] Just think about what an intricate part of our prayer life this profession of our belief in the Holy Trinity is. Before we do anything, before we begin any prayer, we make the Sign of the Cross, proclaiming our belief in the Triune God. At the beginning of the Mass, after the Sign of the Cross, our priest prays, *"The grace of Our Lord Jesus Christ and the love of God and the fellowship of the Holy Spirit be with you all."* again affirming our belief in the Trinity. So think of it, before we even get into the body of the Mass, we have proclaimed our belief in the Trinity *twice*.

During the Mass, when we pray the Gloria, we again profess our belief in the Trinity:

"For You alone are the Holy One,
You alone are the Lord,
You alone are the Most High,
Jesus Christ,
with the Holy Spirit,
in the glory of God the Father. Amen."

During the Nicene Creed, which takes place after the priest's Homily, but before the Eucharistic Prayer, the priest and the people again profess their belief in the Trinity:

---

[1]The Church Teaches Page 123

***The Holy Trinity is the Central Mystery
of our Christian Faith and Life.***

"We believe in God the Father Almighty, Creator of Heaven and earth.

We believe in Jesus Christ, His only Son, Our Lord...

We believe in the Holy Spirit, the Paraclete..."

The Church teaching on the Doctrine of the Mystery of the Most Holy Trinity is as follows:

In God there are three Persons and one Nature (Divine). In Jesus Christ there is one Person and two natures (human and Divine).

The Catechism of the Catholic Church, one of the most powerful books on our Faith, describes the Trinity as the *"central mystery of Christian faith and life. It is the mystery of God in Himself. It is therefore, the source of all the other mysteries of Faith, the light that enlightens them. It is the most fundamental and essential teaching in the 'hierarchy of the Truths of Faith.'*[2]*,"*[3]

Everything begins with the Trinity: God the Father, God the Son and God the Holy Spirit.

The Council of Nicaea (325 A.D.), gave us the Nicene Creed which we proclaim every Sunday at Mass. This Council taught that Jesus was *consubstantial* with God, one in being with the Father. In that prayer, we proclaim Jesus as *"the only-begotten Son of God, eternally begotten of the Father, light from light, true God from true God, begotten not made, one in Being (consubstantial) with the Father."*

Towards the end of the same century (381 A.D.), we were taught *"We believe in the Holy Spirit, the Lord and giver of life, who proceeds from the Father and the Son."*[4]

These few examples we've stated are not by any means all the teachings about our belief in the Trinity. They are just the tip of the iceberg. Woven throughout the history of the Church, as well as the teachings of the Church, we find

---

[2]General Catholic Directory #43

[3]Catechism of the Catholic Church #234

[4]Council of Constantinople

references about the Trinity. The ones we've mentioned are the most obvious, to which the lay community is exposed on a daily basis, whenever we make the Sign of the Cross.

Even before the Council of Nicaea (325 A.D.) which was the first Ecumenical Council, teachings on the Trinity were given us by the Early Fathers of the Church.

In the year 262 A.D., Pope Dionysius of Alexandria wrote in defense of the Trinity, and in opposition to some of the heresies which were running rampant at that time. Part of his letter is as follows:

"For he (Sabellius), in his blasphemy, says that the Son is the Father, and vice versa. But they proclaim that there are in some way three Gods, when they divide the Sacred Unity into three substances foreign to each other and completely separate.

"It is necessary, however, that the Divine Word be united with the God of the Universe; and the Holy Spirit must abide and dwell in God. Therefore the Divine Trinity must be gathered up and brought together in One, a Summit, as it were - I mean the omnipotent God of the Universe."[5]

In the same time frame, St. Gregory the Miracle Worker wrote a short creed, focusing on the Trinity, to counteract the heresies which were attacking the Church. Part of that creed is as follows:

"One God, the Father of the living Word, of subsistent Wisdom and Power, and the Eternal Image. Perfect Begetter of the Perfect, Father of the only-begotten Son. One Lord, Only of Only, God of God, Image and Likeness of the Godhead, Efficient Word, Wisdom comprehending the constitution of the universe, and Power shaping all creation. Genuine Son of genuine Father, Invisible of Invisible, and Incorruptible of Incorruptible, and Immortal of Immortal, and Eternal of

---

[5]Faith of the Early Fathers - Vol. 1 - Page 249

Eternal. And one Holy Spirit, having substance from God and who is manifested - to men, that is - through the Son; Image of the Son, Perfect of the Perfect, Life, the cause of living; Holy Fountain; Sanctity, the Dispenser of Sanctification; in whom is manifested God the Father Who is above all and in all, and God the Son Who is through all. Perfect Trinity, in glory and eternity and sovereignty neither divided nor estranged."[6]

Not to be confused with St. Gregory the Miracle Worker is St. Gregory of Nyssa, who wrote the following about the Trinity:

"It is one and the same Person of the Father by Whom the Son is begotten and from Whom the Holy Spirit proceeds. Therefore and fittingly, there being One Cause of Those Whom He has caused, we boldly say there is One God, since also He co-exists with Them. For the Persons of the Godhead are separated one from another neither in time, nor place, nor will, nor practice, nor operation, nor passivity, nor any of the like things such as are perceived with men, but only in that the Father is Father and not Son, and the Son is Son and not Father, and likewise the Holy Spirit is neither Father nor Son."[7]

It is crucially important that you understand where the Truths which make up our Deposit of Faith come from. We're getting much of it from the Catechism of the Catholic Church, which uses as resource various Ecumenical Councils down through the centuries. These are what we stand on. These Truths make up our Church.

We'd like to share insights from St. Augustine on the Trinity:

*"By the name of God, I now held the **Father**, who made these things, and under the name of Beginning, the **Son**, in*

---

[6]Faith of the Early Fathers - Vol. 1 - Page 251
[7]Faith of the Early Fathers - Vol. 2 - Page 51

Whom He made these things; and believing, as I did, my
God as the Trinity, I searched further in His holy words,
*and to, Thy **Spirit** moved upon the waters. Behold the*
Trinity, my God, Father, and Son, and Holy Ghost,
Creator of all creation."[8]

Now, taking all of this into consideration, all that has
been written about the Trinity, and how much a part of our
Church It is, it's easily understandable why It has always
been, from the very beginning, the subject of major attacks.
The Trinity gives us strength; It gives us power over the
enemy. Thus, it had to be one of the most important Truths
of our Church to be denied, condemned, shoved under the
carpet and destroyed at any cost.

Heresies against the Trinity date back to the beginning
of the Church. But basically, they took the form of:
(1) denying the real distinction of Persons [Three persons]
(Monarchianism, Anti-Trinitarianism and Unitarianism)
(2) denying the divinity of the Second or Third Person [Jesus
and the Holy Spirit] (Subordinationism)
(3) denying the unity of the Divine Nature (Tritheism).

But the biggest problem had to do with the first and
second group of heresies.

We'll list only the most important heresies. But be
aware that these heresies, first manifested in the early days
of the Church, have been with us these many years in other
forms. They've taken on new identities. They're a very
strong part of Modernism and New Age, both from the
Twentieth Century. As we have said many times, the enemy
has not had an original thought for centuries. He takes what
seems to work at any given time and expounds on it, colors
it, re-packages it and gives it back to us.

These are just some of the heresies against the Trinity:

---

[8]Confessions of St. Augustine - Bk 13 - Chapter 5

Monarchianism - Second Century - *denied that there are Three distinct Divine Persons in one God.* They taught that *"God was one in Person and one in Nature."*[9]

Modalism - Third century - Denied the distinction between the Father, Son and Holy Spirit, (making them as one Godhead)

Sabellianism - Third Century - Christ was no different than God the Father.

Patripassionism - Third Century - Taught that because there was no difference between the Father and Son, the Father died in place of the Son on the Cross.

Adoptionists - Taught that Jesus was human, and received divine power from God the Father sometime in his life. This is being taught by many people today.

Monophysitism - Fifth and Sixth Centuries - Taught that there was but one nature to Jesus - Divine - contradicted the Council of Chalcedon who defined the two natures of Jesus, Divine and human.

Monothelitism - Seventh Century - A version of Monophysitism - taught that while Christ had two natures, He only had one will, Divine. - Condemned by the Council of Constantinople.

Nestorianism - Fifth Century - Taught two natures in Christ - one Divine - one human joined together *voluntarily.* Promoted by Nestorius, patriarch of Constantinople and gathered great strength in the Eastern Church. It took until the Fifteenth Century for that heretical group to finally reconcile with the Church.

Arianism - Fourth Century - One of the most deadly heresies the early Church had to fight. It denied the Divinity of Christ, which would of necessity, deny the Trinity and *Theotokos*, the title of Our Lady as the Mother of God. At one point in the late Fourth century, the battle raged, with a

---

[9]Scandal of the Cross and Its Triumph, Pg. 90

majority of the bishops of the world embracing the Arian heresy. St. Athanasius was exiled and St. Jerome stated *"The whole world woke and groaned in astonishment to find itself Arian."* This heresy was condemned at the Council of Nicaea. It was one of the reasons why the Nicene Creed was adopted, to fight the heresy of Arianism. In all its various forms, Arianism was not stamped out in the Church until the end of the Sixth Century, over two hundred years later.

The Trinity is such an important part of the Christian structure that virtually all Protestant denominations believe in the Holy Trinity, and recite the Nicene and Apostle's Creed. They may not give it the same importance as the Catholic Church, but it is part of their Faith belief.

There are some sects and most cults who do not accept the Holy Trinity, even though Jesus invoked the Trinity as He was preparing to leave us. *"Go out and baptize the whole world, in the name of the Father, and of the Son and of the Holy Spirit."*[10]

Any sect who does not accept the Divinity of Christ, or proclaim Jesus as Son of God cannot believe in the Trinity or Sacred Scripture.

St. Augustine spent years trying to understand the mystery of the Trinity. It was during this period of many heresies which questioned the real meaning of the Trinity, that he formulated a treatise on the Trinity which was accepted by the official Church. It upheld Trinitarian theology from that time until the age of St. Thomas Aquinas, who maintained the same Truths as put forth by St. Augustine, but in a way which could be more easily understood and accepted by the Church of the Thirteenth century.

During Augustine's almost twenty years of formulating his treatise on the Trinity, he encountered a boy on the

---

[10]Mt 28:19-20

seashore, who was taking water from the sea and pouring it into the sand. Augustine asked him what he was doing. The boy explained that he was emptying the sea into the sand. When St. Augustine told him that was impossible, the boy responded, *"It's easier for me to empty the sea with this seashell than for you to understand the mystery of the Holy Trinity."*

St. Patrick of Ireland is known to have tried to explain the mystery of the Holy Trinity to the Irish people in a simple way by showing them a shamrock. It is one flower, with three individual leaves on the one stem.

In the final analysis, there has been a controversy going on from the very beginning of the Church about this most important truth and mystery of our Faith. The enemy has tried to cause confusion which in turn would separate Christians. Down through the ages, Christians have tried to understand the mystery of the Trinity. But *it is a mystery*, and by the very nature of the definition, it is not necessary that we understand it, but that we accept it.

When we are welcomed into the Kingdom, we can ask Jesus, and/or any of the great theologians who have spent years of their lives pondering, trying to crack the mystery. But then it won't be a mystery anymore, because we'll be in the presence of the Holy Trinity. And we'll probably all say the same thing that St. Thomas Aquinas said when he stopped writing his Summa Theologiae after having had a vision of Heaven: *"All that I have written appears to be as so much straw after the things that have been revealed to me."*[11]

---

[11]Butler's Lives of the Saints Pg 711

*Jesus chose Peter, James and John to go up with Him to Mount Tabor,
a mountaintop where Jesus would grant them the gift of
seeing Him* transfigured *into His Divine State.*

The Son of the Living God

"Thou art the Christ, the Son of the Living God!"[1]

At this proclamation by the Prince of the Apostles to the Prince of the Universe, the screeches of agony and torment could be heard reverberating throughout the entire world from the depths of hell. The very mountains shook with anger. Volcanoes erupted all over the world, spewing flames from the bowels of the eternal inferno. Earthquakes ripped the earth asunder. Satan and his cohorts could not stand that statement; they shrieked as loudly as they could to drown out the sound and the reality. But nothing they could do, no word, no action, nothing could change the actuality spoken with such great emotion and love by our first Pope: "You are the Son of the Living God." *Jesus is Divine!*

With Peter's prophetic statement, Jesus makes a point of letting him and us know just how prophetic it is. *"Simon, son of Jona, flesh and blood has not **revealed** this to you, but **My Father** who is in Heaven."*[2] In the Catechism of the Catholic Church, they emphasize with italics the two words *"revealed"* and *"My Father"* to differentiate this statement from anything which could come from man.

There are a great many Scripture passages affirming the Divinity of Christ other than this most direct statement by St. Peter. God the Father affirmed the Divinity of Christ in visual as well as vocal terms on two separate occasions. When John the Baptist was with Jesus in the Jordan River, the skies opened up.

"As soon as Jesus was baptized He came up from the water, and suddenly the heavens opened and He saw the Spirit of God descending like a dove and coming down on

---

[1]Mt 16:16-17
[2]Mt 16:16-17

Him.   And a voice spoke from Heaven, 'This is My Son, the Beloved; My favor rests upon Him.'"[3]

And again the Father spoke during the Transfiguration of Christ on Mount Tabor.

"....suddenly a bright cloud covered them with a shadow, and from the cloud there came a voice which said, 'This is My Son, the Beloved; He enjoys My favor.   Listen to Him.'"[4]

Paul wrote about the Divinity of Christ in his account of his conversion on the road to Damascus:

"When He who had set me apart before I was born, and had called me through His grace, was pleased to reveal His Son to me, in order that I might preach Him among the Gentiles..."[5]

Paul had an urgency to proclaim Jesus as Son of God in the synagogues, immediately upon his conversion and for the rest of his life.

"If your lips confess that Jesus is Lord and if you believe in your heart that God raised Him from the dead, then you will be saved.   By believing from the heart, you are made righteous; by confessing with your lips you are saved."[6]

"....I want you to understand that on one hand no one can be speaking under the influence of the Holy Spirit and say, 'Curse Jesus,' and on the other hand, no one can say, 'Jesus is Lord' unless he is under the influence of the Holy Spirit."[7]

And then there is that most famous oath of belief made by St. Paul:

*"But God raised Him on high and gave Him the Name which is above all other names, so that **all beings** in the*

---

[3]Mt 3:16-17
[4]Mt 17:5
[5]Gal 1:15-16
[6]Rom 10:9-10
[7]1Cor 12:3

*Heavens, on the earth and in the underworld, **should bend the knee** at the name of Jesus and that every tongue should proclaim Jesus Christ as Lord, to the glory of God the Father."*[8]

Scripture also affirms that in order to be Christian, we must believe in the Divinity of Jesus.

"The man who denies that Jesus is the Christ - he is a liar, he is antichrist; and he is denying the Father as well as the Son, because no one who has the Father can deny the Son, and to acknowledge the Son is to have the Father as well."[9]

"The Church thus confesses that Jesus is inseparably true God and true man. He is truly the Son of God, who, without ceasing to be God and Lord, became a man and our brother."[10]

St. John Chrysostom, an early Doctor of the Church, affirmed this teaching in one of his liturgies. He sang:

"O only begotten Son and Word of God, immortal Being, You who deigned for our salvation to become incarnate of the holy Mother of God and ever-virgin Mary, You who without change became man and were crucified, O Christ, our God, You who by Your deeds, have crushed death, You who are one of the Holy Trinity, glorified with the Father and the Holy Spirit, save us."[11]

Now, we've spent all this time giving you the doctrine of the Church as outlined in our Catechism of the Catholic Church, the authors of which got their information directly from Scripture. So our belief in the Divinity of Christ is Scripture-based.

Would you think, after all of this corroboration from Holy Scripture, that people who claimed to be Christians

---

[8]Phil 2:9-11
[9]1Jn 2:22-23
[10]Catechism of the Catholic Church #469
[11]Catechism of the Catholic Church #469

could possibly deny the Divinity of Christ? It just doesn't make sense, but sure enough, from the very beginning, there were those who did not believe in the Divinity of Christ. We guess we can accept the Jews and Moslems and Mormons and Jehovah's Witnesses not believing in the Divinity of Christ. They don't believe in our Bible. They don't believe that Jesus is the Messiah. But Christians? Card carrying Christians?

The Divinity of Christ is so key to the Redemption of the world, that it was one of the first and most violently disavowed and attacked Truths and Treasures that we have. From the very beginning, the Divinity of Jesus as Second Person of the Trinity, the Son of God, was challenged. By the very essence of that denial, the Trinity Itself was in effect denied. We, as faithful servants and loyal followers of God the Father, God the Son and God the Holy Spirit, have fought this outrageous heresy from the very inception of our Church down through the centuries to the present day.

Some of the heresies which attacked our Lord Jesus and His Divinity from the very beginning of the Church, are:

Ebionites:

Jewish converts to Christianity *who denied the Divinity of Christ.* Although they accepted Him as Messiah, they believed that he was a mere man.

Simonians:

Simon Magus, and his followers claimed he came directly from the *Divine. The Simonians claimed Simon Magus was the Christ.*

Carpocratians

They denied the Divinity of Christ.

Marcionites:

Marcion's false teachings include the existence of two gods - one good and the other *evil. He denied the Incarnation of Jesus Christ.* He separated Jesus the man from Jesus the

Christ - *alleging that only Jesus the man suffered, not Jesus Christ our Lord, God and man.*

When Marcion asked St. Polycarp *"Do you recognize me?"* he replied: *"I recognize you as the firstborn of Satan!"*

Arianism:

Possibly the most deadly and long-lasting heresy attacking the Divinity of Our Lord Jesus was Arianism in the Fourth Century. It had such long-reaching tentacles that St. Jerome made a statement, *"The whole world awoke and groaned in astonishment to find itself Arian."*[12]

Arianism taught that Christ was not Divine, but was created by the Father to be a catalyst for His divine plan.

You see, to deny one Truth is by its very nature, to deny many Truths. In this instance, if you deny the Divinity of Christ, you must deny the Trinity. If there is no Second Person of the Trinity, there can be no Trinity.

If you deny the Divinity of Christ, you must also deny Mary as Mother of God. If Jesus is not Divine, He is not the Son of God. If He is not the Son of God, Mary cannot be the Mother of God. This is the only logical conclusion you can accept once you embrace that initial heresy. This is why the Church was so adamant, why the Council of Nicaea was so important.

However, even with that, it took centuries to purge the Catholic Church of the wretched effects of Arianism. At one point, at the peak of its greatest strength, Arianism was being embraced by a majority of the world's bishops. It was at that point, in 359 A.D. that St. Jerome made his famous statement about the whole world groaning to find itself Arian.

We have to take a moment here to pay tribute to those great Saints, Apologists, those Doctors of the Church who

---

[12]from "The Proper Context: An Introduction by the Author-from the book "Report from the Synod" by Richard Cowden-Guido - Trinity Communications

fought against the heretics and heresies which have plagued us from the beginning of our Church, very often at the risk of exile from their diocese and country, and sometimes even at the cost of their lives. These have been ongoing battles between the Angels - powers and principalities.[13]

We must take St. Paul's teaching to the Ephesians very seriously. There has been and continues to be a great battle between the good Angels of God with St. Michael, St. Gabriel and St. Raphael in charge of the myriads upon myriads of Angels, against the fallen angels who would drag us down to the pits of hell.

"Put on the armor of God, that you may be able to stand against the wiles of the devil. For our wrestling is not against flesh and blood, but against the Principalities and the Powers, against the world rulers of this present darkness, against the spiritual forces of wickedness on high."[14]

There has been an ongoing battle between the Angels from the beginning of time, and at these crucial periods when Mother Church has fought to uphold the Truths of our Church, the Divinity of Christ, the Trinity, the Scripture and Tradition base of our Church, the Lord raised up great and Powerful Men and Women in the Church to defend His Church. The promise had been made by Our Lord Jesus, *"I will not leave you orphans; I will come back to you;"*[15] *"I will be with you always, even to the end of time."*[16] but it had to be kept by the early Fathers of the Church. Praise Jesus.

Down through the centuries, the attacks have continued hot and heavy. In the last hundred and fifty years, new assaults have been leveled at the Truths of the Church, and

---

[13]Book III of this trilogy, *Cults: Battle of the Angels,* tells about the battles being waged till today with those who deny Christ.

[14]Eph 6:11-12

[15]Jn 14:18

[16]Mt 28:20

in particular the Divinity of Christ. As we said at the beginning, Jews, Moslems, Mormons, Jehovah's Witnesses and the like don't believe in the Divinity of Christ.

Jews are still waiting for the Messiah. They will not accept that Jesus fulfilled the prophecies of the Old Testament. The reasoning at the time of Jesus that He was not accepted by them was because they were looking for a Messiah like David, a military man who, with soldiers and arms would free them from the clutches of their enemies which were the Romans. (That did not happen; Jerusalem was ultimately destroyed by the Romans in 70 A.D.).

Moslems have a problem believing that God could die. They can't accept that God was born as a baby. *"Jesus was born of human estate; Jesus cannot be God. God cannot die; Jesus died, therefore He cannot be God."*

Mohammed *discarded the Incarnation of Jesus.*

He said there is no Trinity; there is only one God.

The Mass is a reenactment of the Crucifixion, Death and Resurrection of Jesus. God could not die. If He could not die, He could not resurrect. It glorified the Triune God in the Creed, which, according to Mohammed, didn't exist. *The Mass had to go.*

The Eucharist is beyond the Moslems' human understanding. It is acceptance of Jesus as God. They do not believe Jesus was God; they believe He was only a prophet.

He said there is no need for the *priesthood.* If there was no Mass, and no Eucharist, why would they need priests?

Mormons: The Book of Mormon teaches that God had a concubine who was Mary, that God had sex with that concubine and she produced two children, Jesus and Lucifer. Jesus is the Son of God as much as Lucifer is. *They don't believe in the Divinity of Christ.* They also believe that men can become gods. Their calling themselves *the Church of the Latter Day Saints of Jesus Christ* is a contradiction in terms.

Jehovah's Witnesses deny the Trinity and the Divinity of Jesus. They believe there is but one God, and condemn the Trinity as pagan idolatry. They consider Jesus to be the greatest of Jehovah's Witnesses, inferior to no one but to Jehovah. Before existing as a human being, he was a spirit creature called the Logos, or Word, or Michael the Archangel. He died as a man and was raised as an immortal spirit Son. His Passion and death were the price he paid to regain for mankind the right to live eternally on earth.[17]

†††

"Thou art the Christ, the Son of the Living God!"

My brothers and sisters in Christ, that's our Faith! That's what we believe in! That's who we are! We've traveled a long road for that belief. We have lived for it, suffered, been tortured, exiled, humiliated and killed for that belief. The war's not over yet. But we have all these Treasures which make up the Catholic Faith. Don't let anyone take them away from you. The cost is too high. We don't exist without them. They're what we hold onto. They're what makes us special, beloved in the eyes of the Lord. *Praise Jesus!*

---

[17]For more on the cults, read: *Cults: Battle of the Angels.*

Sacred Tradition

Tradition is that which makes us who we are and proud of it.

Our grandchildren brought us back T-shirts from a High School Retreat Conference sponsored by Franciscan University of Steubenville in Arizona. It said in extremely large print, **"Proud to be a Roman Catholic."** On the reverse side was printed the Nicene Creed. That's who we are! That's our Tradition! That's what we *are* proud of!

For Catholics, Sacred Tradition is the handing down of Divine Revelation from the Holy Spirit to Jesus to the Apostles, to the Evangelists, to our Popes and Councils, to our Bishops in communion with the Pope, who hand it down to our priests in union with the Bishop who is in union with the Pope, who hands it down to us the faithful.

It's like a great team of players, whether it be football or any other team sport, in which the ball, in this case, the Tradition of our Church, taking their lead from the Head (Jesus working through the Holy Spirit) is passed on, from one to the other, to the other until the entire Body of Christ receives the same message.

The chain of command is critical in the interpretation of Scripture and the handing down of Tradition. Also of extreme importance is that line of authority from Pope and Magisterium, to Bishop, to Priest, to the Faithful. If any of the Hierarchy are not in union with the Pope and Magisterium, rendering their personal interpretation of Scripture and Tradition, they could well be in error, like the good priests-turned-heretics of the past, and what the Body receives is a watered-down, Faith-less, weakened version of the Truth.

Scripture and Tradition are what make up the Magisterium of the Church, the Teaching authority as given

to Peter and the Apostles by Jesus.[1,2] The Catechism of the
Catholic Church tells us:

> *"In order that the full and living Gospel might always be
> preserved in the Church the Apostles left Bishops as their
> successors. They give them 'their own position of teaching
> authority.* "[3]

Scripture is what we read in the Bible; but that was first
orally passed down by those who walked with Jesus; the
books of the Bible were only put on paper by St. Paul in
about 50-51 A.D. and ended with St. John the Beloved's
Gospel in the late 90's A.D. So before the written word,
there was the unwritten, word-of-mouth, handing down of
the Word of God, given to us by the Apostles and Disciples
who had heard the Word of God, lived the experience, and
passed it on. The Gospels were the Word of God taken
from the oral Tradition which, under the inspiration of the
Holy Spirit, were put into a formal *written* form, the Bible.

The writings of Sts. Matthew, Mark, Luke, and John,
Sts. Peter and Paul, James, and Jude are teachings from
these early Apostles based on the Word of God. Remember,
St. Paul, whose writings have been considered possibly the
most important outside of the Gospels, never met Jesus in
life[4]. Everything he wrote was inspired by the Holy Spirit
and based also on the oral Tradition which he heard from
those who had actually been with Jesus or had learned the
teachings of Jesus from the Apostles and Disciples. There
are some passages in the Acts of the Apostles and the
powerful letters of this Saint which lead us to believe that he
had been gifted with apparitions and/or locutions by Our
Lord Jesus in addition to his conversion on the Road to
Damascus.

---

[1]see chapter "Thou art Peter..."
[2]cfMt 16:18
[3]Catechism of the Catholic Church #77
[4]St. Paul had a vision of Jesus on the Road to Damascus - Acts 9:3-7

Another really important point was that the teachings of St. Paul were the first to be written (50-51 A.D.) in what has been accepted as the New Testament. His only reference to what Jesus taught had to come from word of mouth, most likely from St. Mark who went on the first Evangelistic journey with St. Paul and St. Barnabas. We believe this because the first of the Synoptic Gospels, St. Mark's began in 64 A.D. St. Matthew's and St. Luke's were said to be written in the mid 70's A.D.

In the Catechism of the Catholic Church, we read:

"In keeping with the Lord's command, the Gospel was handed on in two ways:

- orally 'by the Apostles who handed on, by the spoken word of their preaching, by the example they gave, by the institutions they established, what they themselves had received - whether from the lips of Christ, from His way of life and His works, or whether they had learned it at the prompting of the Holy Spirit'.

- in writing 'by those Apostles and other men associated with the Apostles who, under the inspiration of the same Holy Spirit, committed the message of salvation to writing.'"[5]

A perfect example of Scripture coming from Tradition is what St. John taught us from the beginning of his first letter:

"That which was from the beginning, which we have heard, which we have seen with our eyes, which we have touched with our hands, concerning the Word of life - the life was made manifest, and we saw it, and testify to it, and proclaim to you the eternal life which was with the Father and was made manifest to us - that which we proclaim also to you, so that you may have fellowship with us; and

---

[5]Catechism of the Catholic Church #76 - Page 24-25

our fellowship is with the Father and with His Son Jesus Christ."[6]

Much of what is written about Tradition comes to us from the Catechism of the Catholic Church, which took many parts of its teachings from the Dogmatic Constitution of Divine Revelation, *Dei Verbum*, from Vatican II. This is what we mean when we say that the line of authority is very critical. Where do you get your authority to say what you say? Our priests and teachers have an enormous responsibility to bring us the authentic teachings of the Church. Even so great a work as the Catechism of the Catholic Church, which we believe was inspired by the Holy Spirit and done under the supervision of Pope John Paul II, never makes a statement without backing it up with either Scripture or Tradition. In the Catechism of the Catholic Church, we read:

"In order that the full and living Gospel might always be preserved in the Church the Apostles left Bishops as their successors. They gave them 'their own position of teaching authority.' Indeed, 'the Apostolic preaching, which is expressed in a special way in the inspired books, was to be preserved in a continuous line of succession until the end of time.

"This living transmission, accomplished in the Holy Spirit, is called Tradition, since it is distinct from Sacred Scripture, though closely connected to it. Through Tradition, 'the Church in her very doctrine, life and worship perpetuates and transmits to every generation all that she herself is, all that she believes.'

"The Father's self-communication made through His Word in the Holy Spirit, remains present and active in the Church: 'God who spoke in the past, continues to converse with the Spouse of his Beloved Son. And the

---

[6]1Jn 1:1-3

Holy Spirit, through whom the living voice of the Gospel rings out in the Church - and through her in the world - leads believers to the full Truth, and makes the Word of Christ dwell in them in all its richness."[7]

"'The task of giving an authentic interpretation of the Word of God, whether in its written form or in the form of Tradition, has been entrusted to the living, teaching office of the Church alone. Its authority in this matter is exercised in the name of Jesus Christ.' This means that the task of interpretation has been entrusted to the Bishops in communion with the successor of Peter, the Bishop of Rome."[8]

So this brings us back to, and affirms what we wrote above, it's crucial that we have that line of authority. Without it, everyone would be interpreting their own thing, and we would wind up with 40,000 some-odd denominations, or as we call them, splinters of the Cross.

Tradition is also handed down, and might possibly come to us in written form, as in the writings of the Early Fathers of the Church, but not necessarily. Tradition consists of customs, teachings and practices which have come down through the centuries. They are usually Scripture-based, but not necessarily. These two strong Truths of our Faith, Scripture and Tradition form the Magisterium of the Church, which is the teaching authority, instituted by Christ and protected by the Holy Spirit.

Scripture and Tradition are both wholly Divine and wholly human. With the aid of the Holy Spirit, tradition remains a rule of belief as it was in the time of the early Church. The Church holds no Truth on the basis of Scripture alone, independently of tradition, nor on the basis of tradition alone, independently of Scripture.

---

[7]Catechism of the Catholic Church #78-79 Page 27
[8]Catechism of the Catholic Church #85 - Page 27

The Council of Trent stated that revelation is contained "partly in written books (Scripture), partly in unwritten traditions (Tradition)." They maintained that "this Truth and teaching are contained in written books and in the unwritten traditions."[9]

The Church accepts three types of Tradition, which are really sequential:

Divine Tradition - Given to the Apostles from Jesus.

Apostolic Tradition - Given to the early Church by the Apostles, which they received from Jesus.

Ecclesiastical - Handed down to the rank and file Church, which had been received from the Apostles.

So you see, it all depended on receiving oral or written traditions which ultimately bring us back to Jesus through the Holy Spirit.

Tradition is the living out of the Gospel through the teachings of the Popes and Councils, the Early Fathers of the Church, and the Treasures we have received through the accepted teachings of our brothers and sisters before us, the Saints. Our Church then consists of the teachings of Jesus in the Gospels, and the living, ongoing traditions which have come down to us these last two thousand years and continue to come down to us through the Popes and the Councils.

To deny the richness of the Traditions of the Church is to deny the working of the Holy Spirit these last two thousand years. It's telling us that the Holy Spirit stopped speaking to the people of God at the end of the Book of Revelation. Pope Pius XII told us that to go back to the early Church would be to deny all that we've been given these last two thousand years; it would be heresy.

The Catechism of the Catholic Church tells us: "'Sacred Tradition and Sacred Scripture make up a single sacred deposit of the Word of God', in which, as in a mirror, the

---

[9]New Catholic Encyclopedia

pilgrim Church contemplates God, the source of all her riches."[10]

Even our separated brethren who claim that the Church has be based on Scripture alone, contradict themselves. The teachings of Martin Luther are what the Lutherans use as *tradition.* They don't call it that perhaps, but that's what they consider it. When Luther began his new religion, he threw out everything except the Bible, and even changed that to suit his needs. But then he came out with all kinds of writings to corroborate and enrich his new teachings. Table Talk is one of the writings of Luther, In 1530, a document called the Augsburg Confession was drafted. It included 31 articles of the Lutheran beliefs, which although rejected at the time, became sort of a Magna Carta of the Protestant Reform. It was picked up in succeeding years by other groups as justification for breaking their ties with the Catholic Church. This became *their tradition.*

In 1548, just two years after Luther's death, a document written by his followers called the Interim of Augsburg, settled an internal dispute in Germany which seven years later, in 1555 became the Peace of Augsburg. This formally recognized Lutheranism as the State religion in Germany with a supporting doctrine, the Augsburg Confession, which basically stated that where the prince lived, he could choose his own religion. In addition, *the Book of Concord* was written in 1580, which formulated the doctrine of the Lutheran religion. But this never had the acceptance of the Augsburg Confession. All of these became part of the *Lutheran tradition.*[11]

Our Catechism of the Catholic Church, which gives us a wealth of understanding, tells us that we are part of the Tradition of the Church, that which is handed down.

---

[10]Catechism of the Catholic Church #97 - Page 29
[11]See Trilogy Book II - Tragedy of the Reformation

"All the faithful share in understanding and handing on revealed Truth. They have received the anointing of the Holy Spirit, who instructs them and guides them into all Truth.

"The whole body of the faithful...cannot err in matters of belief. This characteristic is shown in the supernatural appreciation of faith (*sensu fidei*) on the part of the whole people, when, 'from the bishops to the last of the faithful', they manifest a universal consent in matters of faith and morals."

This is our goal, to be universal. This was Jesus' prayer at the Last Supper.[12] The battle for unity and universality has taken its toll on our Church. It's where the evil one directs his worst assaults. Lately, we read in so many Catholic periodicals or encyclopedias, statements like *"this was the universally held belief until recent years"* or *"this was accepted by the whole Church until the 20th century."* We must fight to maintain our Traditions against those who would overturn them and in the process, overthrow our Church. *Defend our Church. Jesus needs you!*

---

[12]Jn 17:20-23

Mother of God, Mary Most Holy

"When Jesus saw His Mother and the disciple there whom He loved, He said to His Mother, 'Woman, behold your son.' Then He said to the disciple, 'Behold your mother.' From that hour, the disciple took her into his home."[1]

The words highlighted are **Woman** and *hour*. The first time we hear Jesus calling His Mother "Woman" is at the Wedding Feast of Cana when *"Jesus said to her, 'Woman, how does your concern affect me? My hour has not come yet.'"*[2] and the last time is at Jesus' Final Hour. These words, *Woman and hour* appear when Jesus speaks to His Mother at the very beginning of His Ministry, and at the very end.

Mother Mary, as you went over every word your Son ever uttered, did you think about Cana, when you interceded in behalf of the newly-weds, and Jesus changed the water into wine? If you had not reached out to Him, that night, would He have died so horribly on the Cross? As you remembered Jesus' words at Cana did His last words on the Cross take on added pain?[3]

This is the Mother we know, the Mother we love, the Mother who never left her Son's side, right up to His death on the Cross. She is Jesus' Mother; she is our Mother; she is your Mother; Jesus gave her to us.

Most Catholics have a *personal* relationship with Mary, the Mother of God. We believe what the Church teaches about her; but for many of us, she means so much more. For me, she was my first love. I could talk to her; I could count on her. For as long as I can remember, she's always been there for me. She's never left me. I have broken off with her. When I wrapped myself up in the glamour of the world, she stood by and waited. When I thought I had outgrown

---

[1]Jn 19:26-27
[2]Jn 2:4-5
[3]from Bob & Penny's book: *The Rosary, the Life of Jesus and Mary.*

The Mother of God, Mary Most Holy, holding the Christ child

her, didn't need her anymore, she waited. I always came back. She has always been there.

It's important that we understand how important a part of Jesus' life His Mother has been. If God had wanted, Jesus did not have to be born at all. Why did He allow Himself to be born of a *woman* in the first place? Why was the first miracle of His life, God becoming man, accomplished through a *woman*? Why did He choose her, above all the apostles, to stand at the foot of the Cross?

Mother Mary has always played a key role in the Church. She has always been there to help us, to strengthen us against so many adversaries. Those who don't revere her would have us put her on the back burner, downgrade her to the level of a common sinner. We don't believe it's an *intentional* demeaning of Our Lady's role in the Church. They just don't know her the way we do, and not knowing - cannot understand how important she was to Jesus, to the early Church, and how important she is to us.

We pray that we may clearly explain in this chapter what she means to the Body of Christ, *The Church Militant* fighting the battle here on earth. We want to clear up any misconceptions our brothers and sisters in Christ have which would cause them to banish her to such an unimportant level in our Salvation experience. We find it difficult to understand how they think they can know Jesus without knowing His Mother. Let us introduce you to Mary, our Mother, the Holy Mother of God, Mother of the Church.

Let's begin with the very first time we read of Mary in Scripture. The Angel Gabriel said to her, "*Hail, most favored one. The Lord is with you.*"[4]

The Church gives a great deal of significance to this salutation. The phrases, "*Most favored one*" and "*The Lord is with you*" mean that "*Mary is to be the recipient of the Divine*

---

[4]Lk 1:28

Favor, i.e. of the Sanctifying power of God, in view of her office of mother of the Messiah, which the Angel proceeds to announce to her."

"Full of grace" was the term used in all Latin translations of the Annunciation. Lumen Gentium[5] speaks of our belief in Mary's special role in the Church as follows:

"The Virgin Mary, who at the message of the Angel received the Word of God (Jesus) in her heart and in her body and gave Life to the world, is acknowledged and honored as being truly the Mother of God and Mother of the Redeemer...she is endowed with the high office and dignity of being the Mother of the Son of God, by which account she is also the beloved daughter of the Father and the temple of the Holy Spirit."[6]

Mary was startled by the Angel's words. He calmed her.

"Do not be afraid, Mary; you have found favor with the Lord. You will conceive in your womb, and bear a Child, and you will call Him Jesus. He will be great, and will be called the Son of the Most High, and the Lord God will give to Him the throne of David His father, and He will reign over the House of Jacob forever, and His Kingdom will have no end."[7]

"How can this be, since I am a virgin?"[8]

The Angel answered her, *"The Holy Spirit will come upon you and the power of the Most High will overshadow you and for that reason the Holy Child to be born will be called the Son of God."[9]*

The key word in her mind, in her entire being, was ***"The Son of God."*** This Angel was speaking of the Messiah. He was telling her she was to be the Mother of the Messiah,

---

[5]Constitution of the Church; Vatican Council II
[6]Lumen Gentium 53
[7]Lk 1:30
[8]Lk 1:34
[9]Lk 1:35

the Son of God! The Angel further affirmed the power of God, as he added:

"And behold, your cousin Elizabeth in her old age has also conceived a son; she is in her sixth month, and everyone thought she was barren. You see, with God, nothing is impossible."[10]

She looked up at the Angel before her. He was waiting for something, what? Was this messenger of God waiting for an answer from her? Tears streamed down her face. He looked at her with so much love. She gave her answer:

"I am the handmaiden of the Lord. Let it be done unto me according to your word."[11]

We also understand from this historic occasion:

"...It is no wonder therefore that the usage prevailed among the Fathers whereby they called the mother of God entirely holy and free from all stain of sin, as though fashioned by the Holy Spirit and formed as a new creature. Adorned from the first instant of her conception with the radiance of an entirely unique holiness, the Virgin of Nazareth is greeted, on God's command, by an Angel messenger as 'Full of Grace'."[12]

The Holy Fathers affirmed the proclamation of the Dogma of the Immaculate Conception of Mary. The vessel chosen by God to bring the Holy Word, the Son of God into the world, had to be and was indeed free from all stain of sin.

The Church did not first decide in 1854 that Our Lady was born without sin, and consequently Pope Pius IX proclaimed the Dogma of the Immaculate Conception of Mary to all the world. Mary has *always* been known as having been immaculately conceived.

"Through the centuries the Church has ever become ever more aware that Mary, 'full of grace' through God,

---

[10]Lk 1:36-37
[11]Lk 1:38
[12]Lumen Gentium 56

was redeemed from the moment of her conception. This is what the Immaculate Conception confesses, as Pope Pius IX proclaimed in 1854:

"The most Blessed Virgin Mary was, from the first moment of her conception, by a singular grace and privilege of almighty God and by virtue of the merits of Christ, Savior of the human race, preserved immune from all stain of original sin."[13]

A statement made by Cardinal John Henry Newman fits this situation very well: "*No doctrine is defined until violated.*"[14]   There was a reason in the middle of the Nineteenth Century for the Church to proclaim this doctrine. There were historians and theologians at the time who were trying to diminish the authority of Rome in theological matters. One in particular - Johannes Döllinger, a German historian, attacked the Church's right to correct the   research   of   Scholars:[15]   He   defended   Jacob Frohschammer (also German), whose teachings bordered on *Pantheism,*[16] and were declared heretical and condemned,[17] and Czechoslovakian Anton Günther; whose writings were also condemned by theological commissions; but he accepted the Church's position.

There were other teachings which denied the power of the *Supernatural* in the Church; they too bordered on Pantheism, which was growing rapidly during this period.

---

[13]Catechism of the Catholic Church #491

[14]An Essay on the Development of Christian Doctrine

[15]Much like the problem that our church has had with professors in Catholic Universities in the United States whose teachings were not in union with the Church.

[16]Denies the existence of a personal God. Maintains that god is within us and all material things, like the trees and the air, etc.

[17]He attempted to reduce all supernatural mysteries of the Church to natural reason, much like what is being promoted today. Nothing was taken on *Faith*; everything was subject to *natural proof.*

Europe was deeply into the *Age of Reason*;[18] all things Supernatural were being questioned and ultimately denied. Pope Pius IX formally condemned Pantheism in 1861.

We have always believed in Mary's Immaculate Conception down through the centuries, as far back as the Fourth Century by St. Ephraem, St. Ambrose, and St. Augustine, to mention a few - in the Fourth Century, St. Maximus of Turin and St. Andrew of Crete - in the Fifth Century and on and on. The actual feast of the Immaculate Conception was first celebrated towards the end of the Seventh Century.

Pope Pius IX covered all his bases in the Nineteenth Century, and tried to avoid any possibility of controversy by stating:

"The Most Blessed Virgin Mary, in the first instant of her Conception, by a singular grace and privilege granted by Almighty God, in view of the merits of Jesus Christ, the Saviour of the human race, was preserved free from all stain of original sin."[19]

By this statement, our Pope and our Church declared that Mary was given the *grace* and *privilege* through the *merits* of Jesus, not for anything she had done to earn it, but because she would be the vessel through which the Savior would come into the world.

But do we understand? *Incarnation came about!* This is one of the holiest moments in Salvation History, when through the *yes* of Mary, God became God-man, and Heaven was joined with earth. During the Nicene Creed, at Holy Mass, after we profess *"For us men and our salvation He came down from Heaven,"* we reverently add *"By the power of the Holy Spirit He was born of the Virgin Mary, and became man."* This moment is so holy that we are directed in the

---

[18]see chapter on The Sacraments
[19]In his dogma on the Immaculate Conception, *Ineffabilis Deus*

Missalette to bow, and reflect on what happened in a little house in Nazareth, to a Virgin named Mary; and *then* go on to recite the rest of the Nicene Creed. This is the moment when God finalized His Plan, begun in the Garden of Eden, for a virgin to give birth to the new Adam Who *"will strike at his head."*[20]

At this moment, the Salvation of man began, and so we bow in adoration. At Christmas time, we are instructed to kneel in reverence.[21] The next time we kneel is on *Good Friday*, when our Lord gives up His Spirit on the Cross. It has been completed. What began in the womb of our most precious Mother Mary ended with her under the Cross, her Baby Who was born to be sacrificed, dying for our sins. Next Holy Mass, will you bow; will you genuflect?

This is Mary, the selfless Mary we love and honor. We do not worship her; we worship her Son; but out of love for her Son, we grant her the reverence due her, as His Mother. She is truly the Mother of God, as the Council Fathers in Vatican Council II proclaimed. But long before that, back almost 2,000 years, in Holy Scripture, she was proclaimed as Mother of God by a human being, her kinswoman Elizabeth.

As Mary entered the courtyard of the house of Elizabeth and Zechariah, the baby who was to be St. John the Baptist, leapt in his mother's womb. Elizabeth greeted Mary, affirming the words of the Angel, *"Blest are you among women and blest is the fruit of your womb. But who am I that* **the mother of my Lord** *should come to me?"*[22]

Jesus loves us so much, He asked His Mother to stay behind after His death to be with the Apostles. As He hung on the Cross, He gave her to us, when He addressed John, the beloved, *"Seeing His mother there with the disciple (St.*

---

[20]Gen 3:15

[21]Before Vatican II, we would kneel when those holy words were proclaimed.

[22]Lk 1:42-43

John) whom He loved, Jesus said to His Mother 'Woman, there is your son.' In turn He said to the disciple, 'There is your mother.'[23] By this statement from our Savior, our Church proclaims Mary as the Mother of the Church. This was more than Satan could handle. Mary is Satan's greatest enemy.

Is it not strange that Mother Mary would be another part of the True Church, which Jesus founded, that separates us from our brothers and sisters in Christ? And how did that happen! Lucifer, who is the master of confusion, has used the weapon of deceit to spread lies that Catholics worship Mother Mary. Not only is this not the teaching of the Holy Catholic Church, but it is most emphatically not the intention nor the wish of the Mother of our Church. Her words, *"I am the handmaid of the Lord; be it done unto me according to Thy will"*[24] and *"For He has regarded the lowliness of His handmaid."*[25] most exemplify her desired role. She is the moon with no light of her own, only a reflection through which her Son's Light shines, leading *all* the children of her family to eternal life in the Father. Again, we say *all.* Jesus died for all, unconditionally. On the Cross, He did not say *"Here is your Mother."* for only those few who were there, crying for His pain. No, in choosing one of our great Evangelists, St. John the Beloved to stand in for us, He gave His Mother to *all.*

Our Lord having created us, speaks to us and guides us in a manner we can understand simply if we do not let the Satan of pride and confusion block our path to Him. We did not choose our earthly mother, but we can reject her. As with our earthly mother, no, even more than with our earthly mother, although we reject her, malign her, refuse to turn to her, Mother Mary is always present, available, ready to catch us when we fall, hold us in her arms when we feel all alone,

---

[23]Jn 19:26-27
[24]Lk 1:38
[25]Lk 1:48

and lead us to her waiting and most loving Son. This is the Mother we love. This is the Mother we want to share. This is the Mother whom Satan hates.

What is Mary's Role in the Church?

Mary is and always has been *mother.* Her greatest role in our Church is also the last sentence she uttered in Scripture, *"Do whatever He tells you."* No more, no less.

In Oberammergau, Germany, high in the Bavarian Alps, there's a Passion Play put on every ten years. It's the event of a lifetime. The next time it will be put on is in the year 2,000. The play is in German; but the program is written in English as well as German and we are able to follow along very well.

There's a very poignant scene in the play when Jesus meets His Mother on the road to Calvary. The soldiers shove Him along, beating Him with whips. His mother cries out, *"Not Him; do it to me!"* That's who Mary is. Mary is a loving mother who walked behind her Son for the three years of His public life, delighted when He was praised, sorrowful when He was belittled, tormented when He was in danger, and devastated when He suffered and died.

Our Church teaches us that Mary is *"the Mother of the Son of God, by which account she is also the daughter of the Father and the temple of the Holy Spirit. Because of this gift, she far surpasses all creatures, both in Heaven and on earth...She is 'the mother of the members of Christ...having cooperated by charity that faithful might be born in the Church, who are members of that Head.'"*[26,27] She is the Mother of the Church.

The Catechism of the Catholic Church tells us very simply: *"What the Catholic Faith believes about Mary is based on what it believes about Christ, and what it teaches about*

---

[26]St. Augustine - *de Virginitate*
[27]Lumen Gentium - 53

Mary illumines in turn its faith in Christ."[28]   There are no fabrications made about Mary.   We believe - based on Scripture, Tradition and good old common sense.

We know that our Lady was prophetically foreshadowed from the beginning of the Bible in Genesis when God told the serpent,

"I shall put enmity between you and the woman, and between your offspring and hers; He will strike at your head, while you strike at His heel."[29]

Vatican Council II decreed,

"The Father of Mercies willed that the Incarnation should be preceded by assent on the part of the predestined mother, so that just as a woman had a share in the coming of death (Eve), so also should a woman (Mary) contribute to the coming of life."[30]

Life can be beautiful basking in the warmth of Mary. It can be *Heaven, Heaven, Heaven* all the way to Heaven. All she wants is for us to be happy in her Son. She does one thing so perfectly. She loves. Why won't we allow her to love us? There's still time, we pray. But if I were you, I'd open the window of my heart to her right now and let her love shine in, because *Mary is the new Eve.*

---

[28]Catechism of the Catholic Church #487
[29]Gen 3:15
[30]Lumen Gentium 56 *cf* Lumen Gentium 61

The Sacraments

The Sacraments are one of the greatest sources of strength the Lord has given us, major weapons against Satan and his fallen angels. Why do you think the Sacraments have been under attack since the beginning of the Church? You know that Satan is going to try to destroy any of these gifts the Lord has given us because he knows the power they wield.

God loves us so much. These Sacraments are just one more way of Our Lord's keeping the promise He made to us, *"I will not leave you orphans; I will be with you until the end of the world."* He knew we would have needs as individual Christians and also as members of the Body of Christ. He knew we would need strength to complete the journey to Him in paradise. He gave us the means to reach out and touch Him and by touching Him, fill ourselves with His Spirit. ***He gave us Sacraments!***

Sacraments are *"Powers that come forth"* from the Body of Christ, which is ever-living and life-giving. They are actions of the Holy Spirit at work in His Body, the Church. They are *"the masterworks of God"* in the new and everlasting covenant.[1]

The Catechism of the Catholic Church, in quoting from the Council of Trent, teaches that all Sacraments were instituted by Jesus Christ our Lord. The actual passage from the Council of Trent is as follows:

"If anyone shall say that the Sacraments of the New Law were not all instituted by Jesus Christ our Lord, or that there are more or less than seven, namely Baptism, Confirmation, Eucharist, Penance, Extreme Unction,[2] Holy Orders, and Matrimony, or even that anyone of these

---

[1] Catechism of the Catholic Church #1116
[2] Now called the Anointing of the Sick

seven is not truly and strictly speaking a Sacrament, let him be anathema."[3]

"Seated at the right hand of the Father" and pouring out the Holy Spirit on His Body, which is the Church, Christ now acts through the Sacraments He instituted to communicate His grace. The Sacraments are perceptible signs (words and actions) accessible to our human nature. By the action of Christ and the power of the Holy Spirit they make present efficaciously[4] the grace that they signify."[5]

The term Sacrament comes from the Latin and the Greek. The Greek word *Mysterion* was translated into Latin by two terms, *Mysterium* and *Sacramentum*. Later, the Mysterium was dropped in favor of Sacramentum, emphasizing the visible sign of the hidden reality of Salvation which was indicated by the word Mysterium. Thus the Sacrament is the outer sign of an inner truth.

The word Sacrament is the English equivalent of the Latin Sacramentum. Much of what we have been taught about the Sacraments came from the Council of Florence in 1431, the Council of Trent in 1547, and Vatican Council II in 1963.

The seven Sacraments are the signs and instruments by which the Holy Spirit spreads the grace of Christ the head, throughout the Church which is His Body. The Church then both contains and communicates the invisible grace she signifies.

The essential elements of a Sacrament are:

(a) A sensible sign instituted by God, which gives Sanctifying Grace.

(b) Both matter and form present with each Sacrament; the matter is the material used, the form the accompanying words and action.

---

[3]Council of Trent (1547): DS 1601
[4]producing the desired effect
[5]Catechism of the Catholic Church #1084

(c) A minister, (priest, deacon) someone authorized to give the Sacrament with the intention of doing what the Church intends.

The Sacraments are "of the Church" in the double sense that they are "by her" and "for her." They are "*by the Church,*" because she is the Sacrament of Christ's action at work in her through the mission of the Holy Spirit. They are "*for the Church*" in the sense that "the Sacraments make the Church," since they manifest and communicate to men, **above all in the Eucharist**, the mystery of communion with the God Who is love, One in three persons.[6]

The Catechism of the Catholic Church tells us that the Church in the world is the Sacrament of Salvation, in that it is the sign and instrument of the communion of God with man.[7] As Sacrament, the Church is Christ's instrument.

"She is taken up by Him also as the instrument for the salvation of all, the universal Sacrament of salvation, by which Christ is at once manifesting and actualizing the mystery of God's love for men."[8]

The purpose of the Sacraments is to sanctify men, to build up the Body of Christ and finally, to give worship to God. Because they are signs, they also instruct. St. Thomas Aquinas explains the facets of Sacramental signs:

"Therefore a Sacrament is a sign that commemorates what precedes it - **Christ's Passion***; demonstrates what is accomplished in us through Christ's Passion -* **grace***; and prefigures what that Passion pledges to us -* **future glory***."*[9]

All of these Sacraments were under fire at some time in the history of the Church. If you look at the chapter on the Divinity of Christ, you'll see how many heresies there were with regard to that. Most of those same heresies also denied

---

[6]Catechism of the Catholic Church #1118
[7]Catechism of the Catholic Church #780
[8]Lumen Gentium 9, 2 and 48
[9]Summa Theologiae III, 60, 3

some if not all of the Sacraments. In addition to those, there were other heresies such as:

Albigensianism - 11th Century - rejected all Sacraments and Church authority - adopted promiscuous behavior and rejected the state's authority to punish criminals, especially those of the cult.

Berengarianism - Denied the Real Presence of Jesus in the Eucharist.

Renaissance - While Renaissance was not actually a heresy per se, it was a movement which fostered the anti-clerical and anti-Church attitudes which opened the doors for the Protestant Reformation, the Age of Reason and the French Revolution, all of which were very destructive to the Church. To say that the Sacraments were not widely believed or practiced at those times would be an understatement.

Some examples of movements or philosophies fostered in that period which were anti-God would be:

Humanism - begun in the Fourteenth and Fifteenth centuries to give justification to the Renaissance. It advocated giving credit to intellectualism over God or religion. Its form generated a controversy which led the way to the Reformation.

Theological Rationalism - The quest to determine religious and ethical truths by the use of human reasoning, rather than Divine Revelation. To their way of thinking, reason either does away with or supersedes religious faith. They taught that such Catholic beliefs as Creation, Incarnation, Redemption and the like were mythological ideas, having a moral teaching which could be determined by the use of human reason.

Age of Reason - While Renaissance had its strongest support in Italy, the Age of Reason was felt most strongly in France and England. It began with the Scientific revolution which was taking place at the middle of the Seventeenth Century to the beginning of the Eighteenth Century. Reason overtook

Faith and belief in Religious teachings. The movement was supported greatly by anti-Church forces who were able to promote the concept that the Church practiced witchcraft and nonsense, to influence ignorant peasants. Proponents of the Age of Reason gave absolutely no credibility to any of the Sacraments.

Freemasons - Originally started as a worker's guild, it took on strange philosophies including *Deism* and *Theism*, both of which were heretical and denied the Trinity, Incarnation and Redemption. Included in their denial of these Truths were the Sacraments. We will cover Freemasons in more detail in Trilogy Book III - Cults: Battle of the Angels. However, for our purposes here, they were part of the Age of Reason and the Enlightenment.

Modernism - A 20th Century heresy, which had its beginnings in the late Nineteenth Century. It was very strong in Italy, France, Germany and England. It denied everything we believe in. It rebutted Revelation, Scripture and Church Authority. It claimed that Scripture was made up - Jesus never started a Church - He was not Divine - all the Sacraments were bogus. They claimed that St. Paul began the cult of Jesus. We used an analogy in our book, *Scandal of the Cross and Its Triumph* regarding Modernism. It went like this:

"If you want to fight an evil, using the Truths of our Faith: (i.e.) *the words of Jesus and the Dogmas set down over the centuries, and your opponent doesn't want to listen, all he has to tell you is that everything you're basing your beliefs on, is a lie. How do you defend your convictions when your bases in fact are denied? For instance, in Mathematics, we have certain truisms, bases on which to build our blocks. We accept that 2 + 2 = 4; 5 x 20 = 100. But if someone whom you're trying to teach,*

tells you that all your math formulas are false, how do you convince them that they're true?"[10]

Modernism was condemned so sternly and so swiftly by Pope St. Pius X that it seemed like a quick death for the heresy. His decree, *Lamentabiliti*, and his accompanying encyclical, *Pascendi Dominici Gregis*, condemning Modernism, seemed to have sounded a death knell for this heretical group. But as history has proven, it takes centuries to undo the damage done by any particular heresy or heretic. We still feel the rumblings of Modernism in our Church today; in some instances and areas more strongly, and in others not so strong. But it's still there. The dragon is not dead; the dragon is sleeping, *maybe*.

Then we have other religious groups who deny the Sacraments: the Protestant religions, followers of **Luther, Calvin and the like**. We will go into a great deal of detail on these people and how they affected the Church in Trilogy Book II - Tragedy of the Reformation, but suffice it to say that some don't accept the Sacraments as Sacraments; some accept some of them and not others; some of them don't accept the Sacraments as having been instituted by Jesus as we in the Catholic Church believe.

Deism - Heretical group of late 1600's, accepted the presence of a sort of god who existed, and created the world and established certain laws of nature. But they maintained that God was not involved in our day-to-day pilgrimage of life, and rejected any kind of formal religion or religious practices.

Theism - Equates God with every living thing. They don't accept Divine Revelation, but reason. They believe in the existence of God through reason and science. They reject Incarnation, Trinity and Redemption.

---

[10]*Scandal of the Cross and Its Triumph* Pgs 273-274

Pantheism - a heresy which began in the garden of Eden, but which was formalized in 1705 by a former Irish Catholic John Toland. It goes deeper than Theism or Deism in that it maintains that God is part of His creation (Immanence). We believe that God is present in His creation, but not part of it (Transcendence).

All these heresies, denying the Sacraments, the Trinity, the Incarnation, Redemption and various other Truths of our Faith, are all a product of the Age of Reason and Enlightenment, and indirectly, a result of Renaissance. You can see in these movements we've just listed, how human reason has come to the forefront, in place of God and Divine Revelation. It actually began before the Renaissance, but was picked up over the centuries in one form or another, right into the Twentieth century with Marx and Lenin.

You don't have to be a genius to know that this is the work of Satan. As we research one heresy or heretical group, we come upon another. All of them, while differing in some part of their philosophy, have as their main goal the contradiction, discrediting and ultimate destruction of the Catholic Church. We, as a people of God, have held firm in our beliefs in our Treasures, among which the Sacraments are high on the list.

Critics like to say that we use these Truths like a crutch, that we need them to maintain our Faith. We agree; that's true. To even toy with the idea that we may not need any one of these weapons the Lord has given us, is dabbling with the sin of Pride, which can be very dangerous and very destructive. We shake when we hear priests tell us they don't need Miracles of the Eucharist. We beg them to reconsider, explaining that most Miracles of the Eucharist were given to us to reaffirm the faith of priests who had lost their belief in the Real Presence of Jesus in the Eucharist. It's the same with the Sacraments. We need them; don't let anyone lead you to believe that any one of them is not crucial for your pilgrimage to Heaven.

The Council of Trent, 1545-63 was the Ecumenical Council which was involved directly in condemning Martin Luther's errors against the Church. It was a tremendous amount of work because Luther had denied just about everything we believe in. It took a great deal of praying to the Holy Spirit for that Council to be as effective as it was.

In an attempt to put to rest the ravings of the Protestant reformer and his cohorts, thirteen canons were written during that Council with regard to the Sacraments in general. We really think it's important that you have them as a reference. They are as follows:

1. If anyone says that the Sacraments of the New Law were not all instituted by Jesus Christ our Lord, or that there are more than seven or fewer than seven - that is, Baptism, Confirmation, the Eucharist, Penance, Extreme Unction (now called the Anointing of the Sick), Holy Orders, and Matrimony; or that any of these is not truly and properly a Sacrament: *let him be anathema.*[11]

2. If anyone says that these same Sacraments of the New Law do not differ from the Sacraments of the Old Law except in ceremonies and in external rites: let him be anathema.

3. If anyone says that these Sacraments are equal to one another and that one is not in any of greater worth than another: let him be anathema.

4. If anyone says that the Sacraments of the New Law are not necessary for salvation, but that they are superfluous, and that men can, without the Sacraments or the desire of them, obtain the grace of justification by faith alone,

---

[11]*let him be anathema* - This is said after each canon, meaning let the person be cursed for spreading these errors.

although it is true that not all the Sacraments are necessary for each individual: let him be anathema.

5.   If anyone says that these Sacraments were instituted only for the sake of nourishing the Faith: let him be anathema.

6.   If anyone says that the Sacraments of the New Law do not contain the grace that they signify or that they do not confer that grace upon those who do not place any obstacle in the way - as if they were merely external signs of the grace or justice received through faith and insignia, so to speak of a Christian profession by which men distinguish the faithful from infidels: let him be anathema.

7.   If anyone says that, as far as God's part is concerned, grace is not given through these Sacraments always and to everybody, even if they receive the Sacraments correctly, but only sometimes and to some people: let him be anathema.

8.   If anyone says that through the Sacraments of the New Law is not conferred by the rite itself (ex opere operato) but that faith alone in the divine promises is sufficient to obtain grace: let him be anathema.

9.   If anyone says that in three Sacraments, namely Baptism, Confirmation and Holy Orders, a character is not imprinted on the soul - that is, a kind of indelible spiritual Sign whereby these Sacraments cannot be repeated: let him be anathema.

10.   If anyone says that all Christians have the power to preach the word and to administer all the Sacraments: let him be anathema.

11.   If anyone says that the intention, at least that of doing what the Church does, is not required in the Ministers when they are effecting and conferring the Sacraments: let him be anathema.

12.   If anyone says that a minister in the state of mortal sin, though he observes all the essentials that belong to effecting

and conferring the Sacrament, does not effect or confer the Sacrament: let him be anathema.

13. If anyone says that the accepted and approved rites of the Catholic Church that are customarily used in the solemn administration of the Sacraments can, without sin, be belittled or omitted by the ministers as they see fit, or that they can be changed into other new rites by any pastor in the Church, let him be anathema.

†††

The Sacraments

Our Sacraments are broken up into three categories. Baptism, Confirmation and the Eucharist constitute the **Sacraments of Initiation** into the Church.

In the early Church, these two Sacraments, Baptism and Confirmation were administered together. It was considered a double Sacrament at that time. But over the years, the great expansion of the Church, causing many multiple infant Baptisms, the growth of the suburban or rural parishes, and the swell of the size of the dioceses made it virtually impossible for the bishop to be available for all the Baptisms in his diocese. Since the bishop wanted to retain the right to anoint the completion of the Baptism rite, which was Confirmation, the two Sacraments were separated.

Pope Paul VI taught in his Introduction to the Rite of Christian Initiation for Adults:

"The faithful are born anew by Baptism, strengthened by the Sacrament of Confirmation and receive in the Eucharist the food of eternal life. By means of these Sacraments of Christian initiation, they thus receive in increasing measure the Truths of the divine life and advance toward the perfection of charity."[12]

---

[12]Pope Paul VI - Apostolic constitution

The Holy Eucharist completes the Christian initiation. Those who have been raised to the dignity of the royal priesthood by Baptism and configured more deeply to Christ by Confirmation participate with the whole community in the Lord's own sacrifice by means of the Eucharist.

††††

The Sacraments of Healing,
Penance and the Anointing of the Sick

"Through the Sacraments of Christian Initiation, man receives the new life in Christ. Now we carry this life 'in earthen vessels' and it remains 'hidden with Christ in God.' We are still in our 'earthly tent,' subject to suffering, illness and death. This new life as a child of God can be weakened and even lost by sin.

"The Lord Jesus Christ, physician of our souls and bodies, who forgave the sins of the paralytic and restored him to bodily health, has willed that His Church continue, in the power of the Holy Spirit, His work of healing and salvation, even among her own members. This is the purpose of the two Sacraments of Healing: the Sacrament of Penance and the Sacrament of Anointing of the Sick."[13]

†††

The Sacraments at the Service of Communion

The Catechism of the Catholic Church treats the Sacraments of Holy Orders and Matrimony as "directed towards the salvation of others; if they contribute as well to personal salvation, it is through service to others that they do so. They confer a particular mission in the Church and serve to build up the People of God" - Communion.

"Through these Sacraments, those already *consecrated* by Baptism and Confirmation for the common priesthood of all the faithful can receive particular *consecrations*.

---

[13]Catechism of the Catholic Church #1420-1421

"Those who receive the Sacrament of Holy Orders are *consecrated* in Christ's name *'to feed the Church by the word and grace of God.'*

"On their part, 'Christian spouses are fortified and, as it were, *consecrated* for the duties and dignity of their state by a special Sacrament.'"[14]

We have to take a moment out to share a personal testimony. When we made our Marriage Encounter weekend in May 1975, the priest, a saint of a man, Fr. Ted McCabe, whom we had never met before and never met again, shared with us at the Mass. He was hugging the two of us, as we were bathed in tears of joy at the Miracle of the weekend, when he shared with us that our Sacrament was like his Sacrament. We couldn't believe what we were hearing. He repeated it. The Church considers our Sacrament, that of Matrimony, to be on the same level as the Sacrament of Holy Orders.

We were really honored to hear him say that, but we didn't quite believe it at first. Then as the years went by, every now and then, we would repeat that statement at talks, in our books and newsletters, always waiting for someone to tell us we were mistaken. Finally, when we bought the Catechism of the Catholic Church and went to the chapter on the Sacraments, there it was, exactly as the priest had told us. This may be one of the reasons the Church is so against divorce. It is like a priest leaving his Orders. Both priests and married couples are *consecrated.*

We've written short chapters on the Sacraments, highlighting the special assistance the Lord gives us through each of them. You will be surprised when you read them that there are aspects of each of the Sacraments that we're not even aware of. They have been put together by Our Lord Jesus, His Father, and the Holy Spirit, for our well-

---

[14]Catechism of the Catholic Church #1534-1535

being, to aid us through this pilgrimage of life, and bring us closer to our Holy Family here on earth, and when we are preparing for that last journey into the Kingdom. The Catholic Religion is not easy to live by, but it's easy to die by. Well, these Sacraments are the Lord's way of making life easier to live and to die. Take advantage of them. They're for you. They are part of the *Treasures of our Faith.*

I Baptize thee.....

The Sacrament of Baptism

"A voice came from Heaven saying. *'This is My beloved Son with Whom I am well pleased.'*[1] When John tried to dissuade Him, protesting "It is I who need Baptism from You...." Jesus insisted replying: *"Leave it like this for the time being; it is fitting that we should, in this way, do all that righteousness demands."* Jesus, *though He was in the form of God,*[2] was baptized by John! And so when He came up from the water, *"the heavens were opened up and He saw the Spirit of God descending like a dove coming upon Him."*[3]

Baptism is the first Sacrament we receive, opening wide the window of our souls to the Grace of God, welcoming the Holy Spirit to dwell within us. It is the doorway through which the other Sacraments enter. It is the Sacrament of *regeneration* and *renewal* in the Holy Spirit because it brings about the birth of water and the Spirit which Jesus speaks of to Nicodemus, when He tells him that without this *rebirth* no one can enter into the Kingdom of God.[4]

Baptism releases us from the sin, we inherited from our first parents, Adam and Eve - Original Sin. Having received the stain of this sin as a legacy from our first parents, knowing this was through no fault of our own, the Lord with His generous unconditional love, left us the Sacrament of Baptism. While there is much written about Baptism as an important Sacrament of Initiation into the Church, there is not much said about the reason why there is a *need* for Baptism, and what great sin it eliminates. We want to take a moment to speak about the sin of our first parents, that first sin, that of *Original Sin.*

---

[1]*cf.*Jn 3:17
[2]Phil 2:6
[3]Mt 3:16
[4]*cf.*Jn 3:5

Man was created by God in a state of honesty, good moral character. But man, or actually the woman, in this case, disarmed by the wiles of the serpent (Satan), allowed herself and her husband to be dragged down to the level of the snake, and dragged us down with them.

Original Sin is twofold. It is the break with God of Adam and Eve, the first sin that was committed by man. We're told not to dwell on the concept that Adam and Eve disobeyed a direct order from God, their Creator, as much as they spurned God's love and His offer of eternal friendship. They did this of their own free will. They concerned themselves more with *self*, with their own *desires*, and the *lies* of their tempter, than the plan of their Creator. They did not understand that God was only interested in their *well-being*.

*"In **that** sin[5] man preferred himself to God and by that very act scorned Him. He chose himself over and against God, against the requirements of his creaturely status, against his own good. Created in a state of holiness, man was destined to be fully 'divinized' by God in glory. Seduced by the devil, he wanted to 'be like God,' but 'without God, before God, and not in accordance with God.'*[6]

Original Sin came into the world through the disobedience and pride of our first parents. But what resulted as a consequence of their Original Sin not only affected them, it affected us. By Adam and Eve's transgression, they lost the original justice that God had planned for them. But it was lost for us as well (as for them). *"Original Sin for us is the deprivation of original holiness and justice."* It doesn't mean that human nature has been totally corrupted: *"it is wounded in the natural powers proper to it;*

---

[5]that of disobedience to God
[6]Catechism of the Catholic Church #398

subject to ignorance, suffering and the dominion of death; and inclined to sin - an inclination to evil that is called 'concupiscence.' Baptism, by imparting the life of Christ's grace, erases original sin and turns a man back towards God, but the consequences for nature, weakened and inclined to evil, persist in man and summon him to spiritual battle."[7]

The Council of Trent decreed:

*"If anyone asserts that this sin of Adam, which is one in origin and transmitted to all is in each one as his own by propagation, not by imitation, is taken away either by the forces of human nature, or by any remedy other than the merit of the one mediator, our Lord Jesus Christ, who has reconciled us to God in His own blood, 'made unto us justice, sanctification and redemption,'[8] or if he denies that that merit of Jesus Christ is applied to adults as well as to infants by the Sacrament of Baptism, rightly administered in the form of the Church: **let him be anathema.**"[9]*

And so the Lord gave us the gift of Baptism, the first Sacrament of the Church, that which brings us into the Mystical Body of Christ. The term *Baptism* comes from the Greek, *baptizein*, which means to "plunge" or "immerse". Baptism plunges us into Jesus' most precious Heart, and immerses us in the Church which flowed from that Heart.

Baptism bridges the gap between Old Testament and New Testament, between Jews and Christians. At the Easter Vigil Mass on Holy Saturday evening, during the blessing of the water, many Scripture references to water and Baptism are given to us.

a)	At the dawn of creation, the Holy Spirit breathed on the waters.

b)	Crossing of the Red Sea, liberating the Jews from slavery, is a symbol of the liberation given us by Baptism.

---

[7]Catechism of the Catholic Church #405
[8]1Cor 1:30
[9]Council of Trent - Catechism of the Catholic Church #1510-16

c)   Jesus was baptized by John the Baptist in the Jordan river before beginning His public Ministry.

d)   Jesus gave the dictate Himself: *"Truly, truly I say to you, unless one is born of water and the Spirit, he cannot enter the kingdom of God."*[10]

d)   When Jesus gave His mandate to the Apostles, He told them to *"go out and make disciples of all nations, baptizing them in the name of the Father and of the Son and of the Holy Spirit."*[11]

e)   St. Paul teaches that by Baptism, we are brought into communion with the death of Christ. *"Do you not know that all of us who have been baptized into Christ Jesus were baptized into His Death?"*[12]

The form of Baptism is extremely important and well thought-out by the Church.

It begins with the Sign of the Cross, which invokes the Holy Trinity.

[Author's note: Do we ever really consider what we're doing when we make the Sign of the Cross? Has anyone ever explained it to us? We are invoking the Holy Trinity, asking the Divinity to come down and preside over whatever we're doing, whether it be the Mass, or private prayer, or in this case - a Baptism, whereby through the working of the Trinity, a new member is entered into the Body of Christ. It is said in the biography of St. Bernadette of Lourdes that when she made the Sign of the Cross, she did it so so reverently, people made a point of commenting on it. Did she realize, was she given infused knowledge that she was inviting the Holy Trinity into her life, giving God the Father, Jesus the Son and the Holy Spirit Kingship over her soul? Is this what happens to us, every time we make the Sign of the Cross? Is this what happens to the newly baptized, and do we tell them years later of this gift?]

---

[10]Jn 3:5
[11]Mt 28:19
[12]1Cor 6:11

The declaration of the Word of God enlightens the candidates and the assembly with the revealed Truth and elicits the response of Faith from the gathered assembly. This response is an integral part of Baptism.

After the Word of God is proclaimed, the minister[13] pronounces various exorcisms over the catechumen. Then the priest[14] anoints him/her with oil of Chrism, and we hear the priest distinctly renounce Satan. Anointing with Chrism oil is done with three Sacraments of the Church, Baptism, Confirmation and Anointing of the Sick.

The submersion or immersion, or pouring of water on the candidate's head is accompanied by the words "*I baptize you in the name of the Father and of the Son and of the Holy Spirit.*" In Eastern Churches, the following terminology is used: "*The servant of God, N. is baptized in the name of the Father and of the Son and of the Holy Spirit.*" In order for a Baptism to be valid, the name of the Trinity must be invoked. After each member of the Trinity is called down, the candidate is immersed, or water is poured over their heads. Thus the water is dispersed three times.

The person being baptized is clothed in a white garment, which symbolizes that he/she has "put on Christ,"[15] has risen with Christ. The candle, lit from the Paschal (Easter) candle signifies that Christ, through Baptism, has filled the catechumen with His Light and now he/she has been called to become "*the light of the world.*"

Baptism is and has always been such an important Sacrament of the Church that as far back as the Fourth Century, St. Gregory of Nazianzus extolled the graces and blessings of Baptism in his Oratorio:

---

[13]Preferably bishop, priest or deacon, but in an emergency anyone can baptize.

[14]or any of the above in #13

[15]Gal 3:27

"Baptism is God's most beautiful and magnificent gift....We call it gift, grace, anointing, enlightenment, garment of immortality, bath of rebirth, seal, and most precious gift. It is called gift because it is conferred on those who bring nothing of their own; grace since it is given even to the guilty; Baptism because sin is buried in the water; anointing for it is priestly and royal as are those who are anointed; enlightenment because it radiates light; clothing since it veils our shame; bath because it washes; and seal as it is our guard and the sign of God's Lordship."[16]

By Baptism, we become new creatures in Christ. We are truly reborn. We become included as an integral part of the fiber of the Church. Once baptized, one never receives it again. This is why when many Protestant brothers and sisters enter the Catholic Church, they are baptized "conditionally," in the event that they had not been baptized before.[17] But had they been baptized previously, another Baptism would not be necessary.

"Incorporated into the Church by Baptism, the faithful have received the Sacramental character that consecrates them for Christian religious worship. The baptismal seal enables and commits Christians to serve God by a vital participation in the Holy Liturgy of the Church and to exercise their Baptismal priesthood by the witness of holy lives and practical charity.

"The Holy Spirit has marked us with *the seal of the Lord* (*'Dominicus Character'*) 'for the day of redemption.' Baptism is indeed the seal of eternal life. The faithful Christian who has 'kept the seal,' until the end, remaining faithful to the demands of his Baptism, will be able to depart this life 'marked with the sign of faith,' with his baptismal

---

[16]Catechism of the Catholic Church #1216

[17]or had been baptized by someone who is not part of the Christian family

faith, in expectation of the blessed vision of God - the consummation of faith - and in the hope of resurrection."[18]

When a member of our community, be it adult or child, is baptized into the church of God, we proclaim proudly with the Angels and Saint, *"Welcome to our Church. Don't ever leave her."*

Jesus was Baptized in the Jordan River by St. John the Baptist before beginning His public Ministry.

---

[18]Catechism of the Catholic Church # 1273-4

Receive the Holy Spirit.....

St. Augustine being Confirmed by St. Ambrose in Milan, Italy

> *"And in the last days it shall be, God declares,*
> *that I will pour out My Spirit upon all flesh,*
> *and your sons and your daughters shall prophesy,*
> *and your young men shall see visions,*
> *and your old men shall dream dreams;[1]*
> *And I will show wonders in the Heavens above*
> *and signs on the earth beneath,...."[2]*

The Apostles were sitting huddled in the Upper Room. They had deserted their Master when He needed them most. They had been frightened then; they were frightened now. They felt lost. To whom would they turn? He left them too soon. Had it been a dream? How fast it all went, the

---

[1] Acts 2:17
[2] Acts 2:19

excitement, the joy. They were alone! It was over. He had been their strength, their hope, and He was not with them to teach them, to reassure them that everything would be all right. He had told them to wait nine days and the Holy spirit would descend upon them. What did He mean? After all, they were not rabbis; how would they carry on? Doubts and apprehension filled the room; no one dared to voice his fears.

"Suddenly a sound came from Heaven like the rush of a mighty wind, and it filled the house where they were sitting. And there appeared to them tongues as of fire, distributed and resting on each one of them. And they were all filled with the Holy Spirit and began to speak in other tongues, as the Spirit gave them utterance."[3]

Suddenly the fog of fear was lifted and the sun filtered into the room. He had sent His Spirit upon them and they would never be the same! These men who had run from death went out speaking boldly of the Messiah. No amount of threats, beatings, imprisonment could deter them from their mission. *They were evangelists!*

†††

We have seven precious treasures, the Seven Sacraments of the Church, each a perfect diamond in Christ's crown of Glory. Jesus left us His Eucharist so that we would have nourishment for the journey; and sent down His Holy Spirit that we might have courage to live and die for His Church. When we are confirmed, the Holy Spirit descends upon us, just as He did on the Apostles, showering gifts upon us, always ours, ours for the taking, ours for the leaving, but always there for us to take and use.

The initiation that began with Baptism, when our robes were made white, is completed with the Sacrament of

---

[3]Acts 2:2-4

Confirmation; as Catholic Christians we have completed our Initiation into the Body of Christ.

Confirmation is truly the Sacrament of the Holy Spirit. In the Old Testament it was believed that the Holy Spirit rested on the hoped-for Messiah. When Jesus was baptized by John in the Jordan River and the Holy Spirit descended upon Him, this was the sign that He was the Messiah, the Son of God.[4]

Our Lord Jesus prophesied the outpouring of the Holy Spirit on the Apostles and Disciples, on many occasions. And as the Word is alive, and for all time, like God without limitations of time and space, so these words are for us, too.

"...do not worry about how to defend yourselves or what you are to say, because when the time comes, the Holy Spirit will teach you what you must say."[5]

"I tell you most solemnly, unless a man is born through water and the Spirit, he cannot enter the kingdom of God; what is born of the flesh is flesh; what is born of the Spirit is spirit. Do not be surprised when I say; You must be born from above. The wind blows wherever it pleases; you hear its sound, but you cannot tell where it comes from or where it is going. That is how it is with all who are born of the Spirit."[6]

"Still, I must tell you the truth; it is for your own good that I am going, because unless I go, the Advocate will not come to you; but if I do go, I will send Him to you."[7]

"But when the Spirit of truth comes He will lead you to the complete truth, since He will not be speaking as from Himself, but will say only what He has learned; and He

---

[4] Jn 1:33-34
[5] Lk 12:12
[6] Jn 3:5-8
[7] Jn 16:7

will tell you of the things to come. He will glorify Me, since all He tells you will be taken from what is Mine."[8]

"...but you will receive power when the Holy Spirit comes on you, and then you will be My witnesses not only in Jerusalem but throughout Judaea and Samaria, and indeed to the ends of the earth."[9]

The Signs and Symbols of Confirmation

Set me like a seal on your heart. Whenever we sing that during Mass, I think of Confirmation when the Holy Spirit comes down upon us and sets a Seal on our hearts, an indelible spiritual mark on our souls.[10]

The Church attaches a great deal of importance to the signs and symbols which accompany the Sacrament of Confirmation. The Anointing with Chrism is extremely key to the Sacrament. Anointing comes from Biblical times where it had the meaning of abundance or joy; it cleansed and limbered, as in the case of the athletes and wrestlers; it also heals. Anointing with oil makes us radiant with beauty on the day of our Confirmation; as oil cleanses and limbers athletes and wrestlers, so we Christians are cleansed by Baptism and limbered by Confirmation for wrestling with the world with its temptations that pin us down.

When we were baptized, we were anointed with the oil, cleansed from Original Sin and strengthened to lead holy and virtuous lives; with the anointing with sacred Chrism of Confirmation we are sealed with the mark of consecration, anointed *"to run the race."*[11] as foot soldiers of Christ.

The oil used for the anointing is consecrated by the local bishop in the Cathedral of the Diocese on Holy

---

[8]Jn 16-13-14

[9]Acts 1:8

[10]For this reason one can receive this Sacrament only once in one's life.

[11]2 Tim 4:7 *"I have fought the good fight; I have finished the race; I have kept the faith."*

Thursday.   At that Mass, enough Chrism oil is consecrated for the entire diocese for a year.   The major use of this oil is the anointing of the confirmandi.   It is also used for Baptism and the Anointing of the Sick.

Celebration of Confirmation

In order for a catechumen to be officially accepted into the Church, he/she is required to receive Confirmation.

The Sacrament of Confirmation begins with the same form which was used in Baptism, *a renunciation of Satan.* Baptismal vows are repeated. So in a sense, we've gone full circle forming an eternal bond with God, the two Sacraments becoming one in Christ, Confirmation an extension of the Initiation rite begun on the day of Baptism.

The bishop extends his hands over the entire group of *confirmandi.* He prays for an outpouring of the Holy Spirit on the candidates:

All-Powerful God, Father of our Lord Jesus Christ,
by water and the Holy Spirit
You freed Your sons and daughters from sin
and gave them new life.
Send Your Holy Spirit upon them
to be their helper and guide.
Give them the Spirit of wisdom and understanding,
the Spirit of right judgment and courage,
the Spirit of knowledge and reverence.
Fill them with the Spirit of wonder
and awe in Your Presence.[12]
We ask this through Christ our Lord.

The bishop performs the *essential* rite of Confirmation by laying his hands on each confirmandi and anointing him with Holy Chrism oil. As he does this, He says the words,
"Be sealed with the Gift of the Holy Spirit."

---

[12]These are the seven gifts of the Holy Spirit

The ceremony is ended with the Sign of Peace. When we were confirmed, before Vatican II, we walked up to the altar and were given a slap on the cheek by the bishop at the time of the anointing with oil. I will never forget his words: He called me a *"Soldier of Christ."*[13]   That was all I understood of that day - I was now a Soldier of Christ! It still brings tears to my eyes. Little did I know the strength the Holy Spirit was infusing in me; little did I know that my Royal King in Heaven was preparing me for battle. At the time, I did not know the significance of this slap and this commission was to willingly suffer pain and death for the sake of the Church and the Kingdom. Now I know, and for me and my family the answer is yes!

The thrust of Confirmation is the completion of the Initiation ceremony, but on a grander scale; it's adulthood in the Church. It was difficult when confirmandi were twelve and thirteen years old for us as CCD teachers to tell them, or for them to understand for that matter, what we meant by adulthood in the Church.

But Confirmation is also meant to bring us into a deeper relationship with Jesus, to access the gifts of the Holy Spirit, which are now waiting for us, and to make us more a part of the community of believers, the Body of Christ.

Confirmation gives us, in addition to the gifts of the Holy Spirit, a special strength of the Holy Spirit to spread and defend the Faith by word and action as true witnesses of Christ, to confess the name of Christ boldly, and never to be ashamed of the Cross. [This comes from the Council of Florence, of 1439. So the mandate we have been given as baptized Catholics goes back to the early days of the Church, and has been affirmed by a council over 500 years ago.] It's not a new thing; we just have a tendency to forget.

---

[13]That is not done any more.

We have to stop for a moment and reflect on all these gifts we have been given through this Sacrament. There is a key here, upon which all these gifts are based. They have to be understood and accepted before they are received or they don't mean anything to us when we receive them.

We prepared youngsters for Confirmation for five years in our Parish. At that time, the confirmandi were 8th graders. So they fell into the age of thirteen to fourteen years old. We had them for one hour a week for approximately thirty-six weeks, and if you consider holidays, special functions and etc, if we got thirty hours to try to instill in them a love for their Church, an understanding of the role of the Holy Spirit in their lives, and teach them this awesome Sacrament, it was a lot.

We focused on the gifts of the Holy Spirit, so that they could understand what they were receiving and how to use them. It seemed as if we were going over their heads. We tried to make them understand that while the gifts were there for them, they had to take them in order to use them. We used as an example, seven gift-wrapped boxes which we put in the center of the room. We told our students that these were for any of them who chose to take them. Nobody accepted them. Once Bob walked around the room with a five-dollar bill in his hand, offering it to each student. Most refused. About halfway down the group, one young person accepted it and said "Thanks." Bob let him keep the five dollars. The rest of the class was in a rage. Why couldn't they have the five-dollar bill! We explained that this person accepted the gift; they didn't. It's the same with the Gifts of the Holy Spirit.

An order priest from deep in Southern California was giving a mission at our church one year. He began by stating that ours was the only religion that stopped teaching their children after Confirmation. Most of the Protestant religions had extensive training for their people on an adult education level, but the Catholic Church did not. After Confirmation, interest in CCD faded out and as soon as the young people graduated from High school, contact with our Faith was nearly nonexistent. There's a statistic which we were given recently that said that 90% of young Catholics who left high school and entered university, Catholic or secular, stopped going to Mass.

We must change this! Our young people will grow up to be the leaders of our country and our Church. They must be trained how to work toward reward in Heaven as well as on earth, schooled to save their souls as well as they are (schooled) to serve their bodies; the greatest Treasure they will ever have is our Church. But if we are not excited, how will they be? Who will inspire them? To them, what do we represent? They are the Catholics of today and of the next century. Our Church needs them desperately.

We can't take anything for granted. We can't just shrug off what's happening with "*what goes around comes around. They'll be back.*" After only a short time at UCLA, when our son got deep into drugs and left the Church, and rejected all the things we as a family had held dear, he told us not to worry; he'd come full circle; he needed us to come back to. We believed him. We thought it was the only thing we could do. *But he came back to us in a coffin two years later.* We have never taken anything for granted from that time to this.

We are given gifts by the Holy Spirit. They're not just nice words to be used in a ceremony. They're with us for a reason. We must change the world; we must save the world. We can't do it without the help of our Heavenly Family. In this, the gift of Confirmation, we do become *Soldiers of Christ.* We must stand up and be counted. We need the strength of Confirmation to see us through. We love you because we love our Church. We don't want anything to happen to you or our Church. Praise God in all things.

The Holy Eucharist is the Heart and Summit of the Church

(left)
Father Jay Voorhies
Celebrating Mass in our
Chapel
(below)
Father Phil Henning
Celebrating the Holy Mass
with us on Pilgrimage

Pope John Paul II processing with the Eucharist on the Feast of
Corpus Christi - 1979

The Eucharist
The Heart of the Church
Without the Eucharist, the Church is dead.

In the Miracle of the Eucharist of Lanciano, the Host turned into a Human Heart, the wine turned into Human Blood. When we were making the Documentary on Miracles of the Eucharist in Lanciano, Siena, Cascia and Bolsena-Orvieto,[1] the custodian from Lanciano asked us *"Why a Human Heart?"* He explained, *"When the brain is dead, a human is still considered alive as long as his heart is beating. He can be brain dead but he can be kept alive on machines until the heart ceases to beat. When the heart stops beating, there is no life in the body. The Eucharist is the Heart of the Church. Without the Eucharist, the Church is dead. Without the Mass there is no Eucharist. Without the Priest, there is no Mass, there is no Eucharist, the Church is dead, we are dead."*

When Jesus walked the earth, He healed, He performed miracles, He held the crowds enthralled as He spoke of the Father. They hung onto His every word. On the Mount of Beatitudes, He took two fish and five barley loaves, prayed over them and fed anywhere from 5,000 to 15,000 people with 12 baskets full left over. They were excited. They wanted more. They followed Him into the synagogue in Capharnaum where He had gone to pray. Jesus looked upon them with so much love. After all, He was born of them, the chosen people. They were the ones He had come to save. Jesus knew there was little time. Was He, in His humanness, thinking they were ready? Jesus began to teach them the most important lesson of His ministry:

---

[1]For more on these and other Miracles of the Eucharist, read Bob and Penny's book: *"This is My Body; This is My blood, Miracles of the Eucharist, Books I and II."* and order their video series on the Miracles.

*"I am the Bread of life. Your ancestors ate manna in
the desert, but they died. This is the Bread that comes
down from Heaven for a man to eat and never die."*[2]

Jesus identified Himself as the *Bread of Life*, and then
promised *eternal life* to those who eat The Bread of Life.
And then so they were sure to understand, He added:

*"I myself am the Living Bread come down from Heaven. If
anyone eats This Bread, he shall live forever; the Bread I will
give is My Flesh, for the life of the world."*[3]

So that there was no mistake, He referred to *Himself* as
"the living Bread," not a symbol which has no life - *living*
Bread! Jesus went further: *"the Bread that I will give is My
Flesh for the life of the world."* Jesus was not referring here to
a symbol, but clearly stated that the Bread, the *living Bread*
was His Flesh, *real Flesh!*

He spoke of His *Flesh for the life of the world.* How can
this come about, except through the ongoing Sacrifice of the
Mass which brings us His Flesh in the Eucharist? In that
same verse, was Jesus not promising to be with us till the end
of the world *(or the life of the world)?* Is it not through the
Mass that Jesus intended and intends to keep His promise
not to leave us orphans? How else could He remain with
us? Is this why, knowing His time was short and desiring to
be with them till the end of time, He had the urgency to
teach them about the Eucharist?

Upon hearing this, the Jews quarreled among
themselves. Determined, Jesus persisted:

*"Let Me solemnly assure you, if you do not eat the Flesh of
the Son of Man and drink His Blood, you have no life in you."*[4]

He could see them beginning to scatter. He had to
reach them! He stressed over and over again that unless
they ate His Flesh and drank His Blood they would have no

---

[2]Jn 6:48-50
[3]Jn 6:51
[4]Jn 6:53

life in them, and without this, they would not have eternal life. Imagine the wounds to His Sacred Heart, seeing their stubborn minds and stony hearts, blinding them to His Gift to them, the Gift of Himself for all eternity. They wanted to be freed from the Romans. He promised them freedom from sin. Had He not shown them that true healing comes about through forgiveness of sin! Did they not hear His message: When sin is defeated in the world, persecution and tyranny will die as well - that this was why He was born; this is why He would die?

"For My Flesh is real food and My Blood real drink."[5]

What was Jesus saying? You do not *gnaw*[6] on symbols! Lest they misunderstood, Jesus further stressed that the Eucharist *was not* a symbol, by repeating The Eucharist was His *Flesh* and then to further emphasize the point - real food and drink.

In case we who have followed have a problem understanding Jesus' intent, He continued:

"The man who feeds on My Flesh and drinks My Blood remains in Me, and I in him."[7]

The Lord used the word *feed* or as it was in the original Aramaic - gnaws! There is no question but that He was speaking about *Real Flesh* and *Real Blood*. You do not feed on symbols; you do not drink symbols. He promised that those who partake of His Flesh and Blood would remain in Him and He in them. It is only in the Catholic Church, under His Vicar, direct descendant from the first Pope Peter[8] that this unity can and does come about, at the ongoing Sacrifice of the Cross, the Mass.

---

[5]Jn 6:55

[6]Jn 6:54-58 footnote in New American Bible - The verb John uses in these verses is not the regular verb "to eat," but a very realistic, very graphic "*to munch, to gnaw.*"

[7]Jn 6:56

[8]Read the chapter on the Authenticity of the Popes in this book

Jesus promised eternal life when He told the Jews:

"Unlike your ancestors who ate and died, whoever eats this Bread will live forever."[9]

Jesus, sensing His words were too hard for the Jews to bear, asked *"Does this shake your faith?"*[10] Now, He had walked among them, fed them, healed them, filled them with the word of the Father. Now, Jesus was asking them to trust in Him and His Word. Well, we all know what happened then. First they murmured among themselves and then they left.

But before we judge the Jewish people we must remember that according to the Law of Moses, Jews were not allowed to drink *animal* blood. What we consider pink, juicy (rare or medium-rare) steak, would constitute to a Jew the drinking of animal blood. According to the Kosher laws of Moses, meat must be soaked in water or salted so that no blood remains. Now no longer looking on Jesus as possibly the Messiah but instead *"that Nazarene,"* they rejected Him.

Jesus spoke of eating His *Flesh.* Now, in the Judean Hills there were tribes practicing cannibalism. To the Jews Jesus was suggesting cannibalism. He knew His people. He knew what they were thinking? Why didn't He say, *I didn't mean My Flesh; it's only a symbol?* No one would have left. He had an urgency. He knew He had so little time. Why didn't he say it was a symbol? Because it **isn't** and **never was** a symbol, but His Flesh and Blood of which they were to partake in a *non-cannibalistic* way. And yet, our brothers and sisters in Christ, from whom we are separated, claim the Host is merely a symbol!

His sermon on the Eucharist was a gift! Jesus took a chance on His people; He saw them as they could be, if they accepted the whole Truth. Make no mistake about it, He

---

[9]Jn 6:58
[10]Jn 6:59

loved the Jews; He loves the Jews; He died for the Jews as well as those who would believe in Him. He loved them so, He wanted to remain with them, to help them on their journey which we know would get so rocky many would fall[11] at the hands of men deluded by Lucifer. He was telling them *how* He could remain with them.

This Discourse on the Bread of Life was so important to Jesus, He even turned to the Apostles and asked them if they would leave Him also. He was ready to let the last of His followers go, the Eucharist was so important!

Jesus knew how frail were those He was leaving behind, to carry on His Mission. Our early Church Fathers said, the Church (He founded) would not have lasted 100 years without the Eucharist, Jesus the God-man among them in His Body, Blood, Soul and Divinity. Why was (and is) the Eucharist so important to the life of the Church? Because the Eucharist is Jesus with us! It was Jesus Who saved the early Church, and true to His promise it is He Who is saving her now and will till the day He returns.

Jesus also knew the tool of Pride that Lucifer would use against His Church, how some would put themselves above the Word of God. Just as God the Father in the Old Testament, Jesus chose to work with the *few* who would believe and later die a martyr's death for that belief. Jesus wanted it to be clearly known that it Was He, present in the Eucharist who would save the Church. This handful of Apostles and Disciples were to be reminiscent of what God said to Gideon,

"'You have too many soldiers with you for Me to deliver Midian unto their power, lest Israel vaunt against me and say 'My own power brought me the victory.' Now proclaim to all the soldiers, If anyone is afraid or fearful, let him leave."[12]

---

[11]the Holocaust during World War II where 6,000,000 Jews would be killed in concentration camps.

[12]Judg 7: 2-4

"When Gideon put them to the test on the mountain, **twenty-two thousand** of the soldiers left, but **ten thousand** remained. The Lord said to Gideon, *'There are still too many soldiers. Lead them down to the water and I will test them for you there'*...When Gideon led the soldiers down to the water, the Lord said to him *'You shall set to one side everyone who laps up the water as a dog does with its tongue; to the other, everyone who kneels down to drink.'*

"Those who lapped up the water raised to their mouths by hand numbered **three hundred**, but all the rest of the soldiers knelt down to drink the water. The Lord said to Gideon, *'By means of the three hundred who lapped up the water I will save you and will deliver Midian into your power. So let all the other soldiers go.'"*[13]

To recap this story, out of **twenty-two thousand**, the Lord allowed Gideon *three hundred,* by which the Midian forces of **one hundred thirty five thousand** soldiers were destroyed. The Lord would not allow them for one moment to think they had anything to do with the victory. It was totally the power of God. The same applied to the twelve apostles of Jesus.

†

The Last Supper

Let us try to place ourselves in the Upper Room. Jesus is about to suffer His Agony in the Garden, be rejected by those He had come to save, be deserted and denied by those He had chosen, be scourged mercilessly at the Pillar, be mocked as soldiers cruelly pierce His precious Head with a crown of thorns, fall three times under the weight of the Cross, encounter His Mother and her greatest pain - seeing her Son suffer and die most horribly on the Cross. And with all of this before Him, His thoughts are of us, how He can be with us, not leave us orphans.

---

[13]Judg 7:22

The Eucharist was extremely important to Jesus. Knowing all He was to suffer that night and the next day, His Passion and Death on the Cross, He instituted the Mass at the Last Supper. He had spoken of the Eucharist at Capharnaum[14] and now before leaving them, He would show them *how* He would not leave them orphans, *how* they would have Him with them till the end of the world. When He had tried to prepare them for His suffering and death, they could not bear it. Little did they realize this was crucial, if the Gates of Heaven were to open. They could not understand that the Last Supper Jesus was celebrating with them would lead to His Sacrifice of the Cross.

"Then taking bread and giving thanks, He broke it and gave it to them, saying: 'This is My Body to be given for you. Do this as a remembrance of Me.' He did the same with the cup after eating, saying as He did so: 'This cup is the new covenant in My Blood, which will be shed for you.'"[15]

Although they would run and not be with Him when He suffered and died on the Cross, every time they celebrated this Last Supper *"in remembrance of Him,"* they would be with Him, they would be a part of the ongoing Sacrifice of the Cross, the Sacrifice of Mass.[16] For 2000 years and beyond, they and those who would come after them, would join Jesus the Victim-Priest in Heaven, offering an ongoing Sacrifice to God the Father "in persona Christi Capitas," in the person of Christ.

The Disciples on the Road to Emmaus

It was so important to Jesus that those whom He had left behind understand the place of the Eucharist in their lives, one of the first things He did after He rose from the dead was affirm the Eucharist. There were two disciples

---

[14]Jn 6:51
[15]Lk 22:19
[16]Council of Trent

walking on the roadside to Emmaus, approximately seven miles from Jerusalem. As they walked dejectedly, discussing all that had transpired in Jerusalem, who should they encounter but a stranger. He asked them what they had been discussing. Distressed, they turned to Him and said:

"Are you the only resident of Jerusalem who does not know the things that went on there these past few days?"[17]

They told Him all that had happened, how they had thought that Jesus was the Messiah, the Anointed one, that He would free them from enslavement by the Romans, and the chief priests and elders had killed Him. All they had hoped for was lost. Then the Stranger explained how all this had to happen so that *"the Messiah could enter into His glory."*[18] He went through Holy Scripture showing them all the passages that had been fulfilled by the Messiah, and how all that had come to pass with Jesus had been foretold by the prophets. They came to the end of the road and the Stranger acted as if He were going on. They pressed Him to stay with them, as it was getting late. They sat down. He took bread; broke it, pronounced the blessing and passed the bread to the others. With that, their eyes were opened and they recognized that it was Jesus, whereupon He disappeared.

As they returned hurriedly to Jerusalem to tell the Apostles what had happened, they said to one another,

"Were not our hearts burning, as He talked to us on the road and explained the Scriptures to us?"[19]

But they recognized Him in the breaking of the bread! How often we hear our brothers and sisters in Christ say they are *Church shopping.* Their hearts burn when they hear a minister preaching the Good News, but then they hunger for more and they continue searching, going from church to

---

[17]Lk 24:18
[18]Lk 24:26
[19]Lk 24:32

church, never realizing what they are yearning for is Jesus Present in the Eucharist.

Have you ever had a Fundamentalist ask: "*Is Jesus your personal Savior*?" How more *personal* a Savior can He be than when Jesus comes to dwell in us through the Eucharist? One of our priest friends told a Fundamentalist "He is not only my Personal Savior; *He is my Intimate Savior.* I am nourished by His Body and Blood every day."

We no longer loving, but He loving through us; we no longer listening, but He listening through us; we no longer feeding the hungry, but He feeding through us; we no longer mending the broken hearts of our brothers and sisters, but He mending through us.

As St. Paul wrote "*...yet I live, no longer I, but Christ lives in me.*"[20]

St. Augustine the great Doctor of the Church and convert said that when we receive Communion, we do not consume Jesus; Jesus consumes us. If we accept this Grace from the Lord, then we no longer live but Jesus lives in us. He has called us by name and made us His own. And we will never be the same. This is the reason we need the Sacrament of Penance. Would we want the Lord to enter a filthy house and dwell therein?[21]

†††

The Catechism of the Catholic Church gives many titles to the Sacrament of the Eucharist:

Eucharist - thanksgiving to God, for the gift of union with Him, for the gift of Life! The Jewish people would give thanks to God, especially during a meal.

The Lord's Supper - so called because of its direct connection with the Last Supper which the Lord took with the Apostles and Disciples. It was at this time that He

---

[20]Gal 2:20

[21]Read about this life-giving Sacrament in another chapter

instituted the Eucharist, the Mass, and the Priesthood; it was at the *Seder*, the meal of the Passover when Jews recall their *Exodus*, their release from the captivity of the Egyptians; at the Lord's Supper Jesus will give us the Eucharist, the means to free us from the captivity of sin.

The Breaking of the Bread - According to Scripture, when Jesus gave us His *Body, Blood, Soul and Divinity* during the Last Supper, He did it *as part of a Jewish meal, as master of His table.*[22] Each of the synoptic Gospel writers recorded this event.[23] This is how the disciples will recognize Him, *in the breaking of the bread*, when they encounter Him in Emmaus, after He rises from the dead.

The Eucharistic Assembly - This expression is used *"because the Eucharist is celebrated amid the assembly of the faithful, the visible expression of the Church."*

The **memorial** of the Lord's Passion and Resurrection.

The Holy Sacrifice - The terms *Holy Sacrifice of the Mass, Sacrifice of Praise, Spiritual Sacrifice, pure and holy Sacrifice* are also used.

The Holy and Divine Liturgy - because the Church's whole liturgy finds its center and most intense expression in the celebration of this Sacrament.

Most Blessed Sacrament - because it is the Sacrament of Sacraments. The Eucharistic Species reserved in the Tabernacle is also called the Most Blessed Eucharist.

Holy Communion - because by this Sacrament we unite ourselves to Christ, Who makes us sharers in His Body and Blood to form one single body.

The Bread of Angels,

---

[22]Catechism of the Catholic Church #1329
[23]Mt 26:26-29; Mk 14:22-25; Lk 22:19 -20;1Cor 11:24

Bread from Heaven,
Medicine of immortality,
Viaticum

Holy Mass - because the liturgy in which the mystery of Salvation is accomplished concludes with the sending forth (missio) of the faithful, so that they may fulfill God's will in their daily lives.

The Eucharist - Communion - Unity

The Eucharist - *"Holy Communion is an intimate union with Christ Jesus."*[24] - union - He living in us and we in Him.

"The man who feeds on My Flesh and drinks My Blood, remains in Me, and I in him."[25]

Through the reception of the Eucharist during the Sacrifice of the Mass, we become one in Him as He is one with the Father. Jesus said:

"Just as the Father who has life sent Me and I have life because of the Father, so the man who feeds on Me will have life because of Me."[26]

Communion signifies also our unity with the teaching of the Church, with the successor of Peter and his bishops and the unity that comes about with the rest of the assembly. This is why brothers and sisters who are not part of the Roman Catholic Church are not allowed to partake of the Eucharist in our church. They have not accepted the Community of Christ. They are most welcome to share in the Word and all the parts of the Mass; but receiving the Eucharist is reserved only to those who are in *communion* with the Pope and His Church, who believe in and accept all the tenets of the Faith, the Creed, the Magisterium and pledge of obedience to the successor of Peter, the Pope. This is the Community of God, the Church Militant.

---

[24]Catechism of the Catholic Church #1391
[25]Jn 6:56
[26]Jn 6:57

*"The Eucharist is the efficacious (*effective*) sign and sublime cause of that communion in the Divine life and that unity of the People of God by which the Church is kept in being. It is the culmination both of God's action sanctifying the world in Christ and of the worship men offer to Christ and through Him to the Father in the Holy Spirit."[27]*

Here in this section of the Catechism of the Catholic Church, we read that which we have always believed from the very beginning, that it is through the presence of Jesus in our midst, the Eucharist, that we have that union between Heaven and earth and through that union the Church has survived 2000 years of persecution, in one form or the other. It is through that union that hell has not prevailed against Christ's Church.

"The unity of the Mystical Body: the Eucharist makes the Church. Those who receive the Eucharist are united more closely to Christ. Through it Christ unites them to all the faithful in one body - the Church. Communion renews, strengthens, and deepens this incorporation into the Church, already achieved through Baptism. In Baptism we have been called to form but one body. The Eucharist fulfills this call: 'The cup of blessing we bless, is it not a participation in the Blood of Christ? The Bread which we break, is it not a participation in the Body of Christ? Because there is one Bread, we who are many are one body, for we all partake of the one Bread.'"[28] [29]

St. Paul, in this letter to the Corinthians states plainly that the cup is *Blood* and the Bread is the *Body* of Christ. He goes on to say that it is through the partaking of that one Loaf, the sharing of the Body and Blood of Christ, the Eucharist, that we are one body (unity).

---

[27]Catechism of the Catholic Church #1325
[28]1Cor 10:16,17
[29]Catechism of the Catholic Church #1396

"At the Last Supper, on the night He was betrayed, our Savior instituted the Eucharistic sacrifice of His Body and Blood. This He did in order to perpetuate the Sacrifice of the Cross throughout the ages until He should come again, and so entrust to His beloved Spouse, the Church, a memorial of His death and resurrection: a Sacrament of Love, a sign of unity, a bond of charity, a Paschal banquet in which Christ is consumed, the mind is filled with grace, and a pledge of future glory is given to us."[30]

What was required for our salvation was the Sacrifice of the Perfect Lamb, the Son of God - Our Lord Jesus, the Sacrifice that took place and was culminated on the Cross. The Eucharist comes to us through the ongoing Sacrifice of the Cross, the Sacrifice of the Mass where the victim-priest *"in persona Christi"* offers sacrifice to the Father, doing it in remembrance of Him, as Jesus commanded the night of the Last Supper. And it is through the Eucharist that man is saved and has eternal life.

There are those who say that the Eucharist is not more important than the other three elements in the Mass: the Word, the Priest, the assembly. This is an error and not according to Catholic Theology. Again the Catechism of the Catholic Church states:

"The Eucharist is the source and summit of the Christian life. The other Sacraments, and indeed all ecclesiastical ministries and works of the apostolate, are bound up with the Eucharist and we are oriented toward it. For in the Blessed Eucharist is contained the whole spiritual good of the Church, namely Christ Himself, our Pasch (Passover)."[31]

What was the Catechism of the Catholic Church saying when it reads the source of Christian life? We looked up the

---

[30]Catechism of the Catholic Church #1323

[31]Catechism of the Catholic Church #1324 - from St. Irenaeus

word *source*. We found the word - author: Is Jesus not the *Author* of Life? As Creator, did not the Trinity (Father, Son and Holy Spirit) create our world? At the moment of *conception*, did not Jesus incarnate and God became man? Source also means *foundation*. Did not Jesus call Himself the *corner stone*?

The other word that caught our hearts was *summit*. Looking it up, we found words like: *pinnacle, height, epitome, apex*. When you place these adjectives in front of Christian life, you begin to see the impact that the Eucharist has in the living out of our Christian life on earth. The *Pinnacle* of Christian Life? The Catechism and the Church has taught for 2000 years that all the Sacraments revolve around the Eucharist, the most important of all.

"each particular Sacrament has its own vital place. In this organic whole, the Eucharist occupies a unique place as the "Sacrament of Sacraments:" all the other Sacraments are ordered to it as to their end."[32]

"...they (the Sacraments) *manifest and communicate to men, above all in the **Eucharist**,[33] the mystery of communion with God Who is love, One in Three Persons.*[34]

The Eucharist, the Heart of our Church

In the Catechism of the Catholic Church it states:
Holy Mass - *"...the liturgy in which the mystery of Salvation is accomplished."*[35]

The Eucharist is *"**the** most important part of our Church."* The Eucharist as the Source and Summit of Ecclesial life is taken from Lumen Gentium,[36] a proclamation of Vatican

---

[32]Catechism of the Catholic Church #1211 - from St. Thomas Aquinas

[33]the author made this bold

[34]Catechism of the Catholic Church #1118

[35]Catechism of the Catholic Church #1332

[36]Lumen Gentium 11:6 - "Taking part in the Eucharistic Sacrifice, which is the *fount* and *apex* of the whole Christian life"

Council II, promulgated by Pope Paul VI on November 21, 1964, and yet there are those within and without the Church, with hearts of stone who wound our Lord by refusing to be one with Him in the Eucharist. As He did on the Cross, so now He opens His Arms and waits to embrace us.

This is one of the reasons we're writing these books, to give you something to hold on to, to turn to in time of doubts and attacks. We have researched many years to bring you something you can read and hold onto which confirm what we have always believed, to put your hands on the doctrines which authenticate the Truths passed on to us by Apostles after Apostles, from faithful to faithful. We pray that these books will give you strength to fight for your Church, so that those who see and hear you will say, "*If it means that much to them, it must be the True Church!*" When you have an urgency to confirm that *what you know, or think you know, or want to know* about our Church is solid doctrine, look at the footnotes, at the resources we are using to bring you this material. Everything is approved by the Magisterium, the teaching authority of the Church, which it uses to form the Deposit of Faith. We've even taken to buying a Code of Canon Law, a Sacramentary and a Roman Missal, so that we can look up what we're supposed to believe in and *stand on those Truths.*

Another reason we use these resources, why we quote from these references used in the Catechism of the Catholic Church which were written anywhere between twenty and thirty years ago, and are part of Vatican Council II, is because we want you to be aware that the Church *has not changed* their views on the Eucharist due to Vatican Council II, or in the so-called "*Spirit of Vatican Council II.*"[37] The English version of the Catechism of the Catholic Church was

---

[37]many abuses have been fostered in the name of the spirit of Vatican Council II which are nothing more than taking the documents and twisting them to individual agendas

published in 1994. The quotations we've used here are from that Catechism. It answers many questions.

●Do we believe that Jesus is truly, really Present in the Eucharist, Body, Blood, Soul and Divinity?

●Is the Host truly the Body and Blood of Christ, no longer bread?

●Is the Cup truly the Blood of Christ, no longer wine?

●Is Christ *totally* present - Body, Blood, Soul and Divinity in the consecrated Host and *equally, totally* present in the Blood in the chalice - the whole Christ, *Body, Blood, Soul and Divinity?*

●Is Jesus truly present in the Eucharist - *Body, Blood, Soul and Divinity* - reserved in the Tabernacle after the Mass has ended?

●Is the Sacrifice of the Mass, the ongoing Sacrifice of the Cross?

●Does the Catechism of the Catholic Church teach, and the Catholic Church promote Eucharistic Adoration?

●Is Heaven an actual place?[38]

●Does the Church still teach about Heaven, Hell and Purgatory?[39]

The answers to all of the above and many many other questions you have is a resounding *Yes!* and these answers can all be found in the Catechism of the Catholic Church, with references as to where *they* got their information.

†††

The Catechism of the Catholic Church explains Christ's Presence in the Eucharist in a unique way:

---

[38]As the New Catholic Encyclopedia states,

"Because Christ and Our Lady are now glorified in Body and because a body requires a place in which to dwell, Church tradition, following the language of Scripture, has constantly taught that Heaven is a place."

[39]Read Bob & Penny's book: *Heaven, Hell and Purgatory.*

"Christ Jesus, who died, yes, who was raised from the dead, who is at the right hand of God, who indeed intercedes for us, is present in many ways to His Church: in His Word, in His Church's prayer, 'where two or three are gathered in My Name,' in the poor, the sick, and the imprisoned, in the Sacrifice of the Mass, and in the person of the minister. But 'He is present...most *especially in the Eucharistic Species.*'"

"The mode of Christ's Presence under the Eucharistic Species is unique. It raises the Eucharist above all the Sacraments as 'the perfection of the Spiritual life and the end to which all Sacraments tend.' In the Most Blessed Sacrament of the Eucharist 'the Body and Blood, together with the Soul and Divinity, of our Lord Jesus Christ and, therefore, *the whole Christ is truly, really and substantially contained.*"[40] **So much for those who say the Eucharist is a Symbol or not any more important than the Word, the Minister or the Congregation.**

The Catechism of the Catholic Church continues:

"This Presence is called *'real'* - by which is not intended to exclude the other types of presence as if they could not be 'real' too, but because it is presence in the fullest sense: that is to say, it is a substantial Presence by which Christ, God and man, makes Himself wholly and entirely present."[41]

Our Church is so exciting, isn't she? We are so filled with riches and Treasures. Nothing has been taken away from us. Don't let anyone take anything away from you. Take the time to find out. It's so important for Catholics today to know that what we were taught all those many years ago are still on the books; they are still part of the Deposit of Faith.

The Real Presence is brought about by Transubstantiation. The Catechism quotes the Council of Trent who defines Transubstantiation as follows:

---

[40]Catechism of the Catholic Church - #1373 - #1374
[41]Pope Paul VI - *Mysterium Fidei*

"Because Christ our Redeemer said that it was truly His Body that He was offering under the Species of bread, it has always been the conviction of the Church of God, and this holy Council now declares again, that by the Consecration of the bread and wine there takes place a change of the whole substance of the bread into the Substance of the Body of Christ our Lord and of the whole substance of the wine into the Substance of His Blood. This change the holy Catholic Church has fittingly and properly called Transubstantiation."[42]

In the Catechism of the Catholic Church, verification of the presence of Jesus in the Eucharist in the Tabernacle is affirmed,[43] and Eucharistic Adoration is recommended.[44] The Catechism also tells us that the Eucharist is to be worshiped with the worship of *latria* - Praise due to God alone.[45] How can anyone not adore You, Lord, knowing that is You really present? Thank you for the grace to believe.

In Holy Communion, the whole Christ is received under either Species. The Catechism[46] professes that when we receive Jesus in the Host, we are receiving the entire Jesus, Body, Blood, Soul and Divinity, and that form is what has become the usual form of receiving Communion. This is also confirmed by the *decree regarding Communion under Both Species and Communion to Children,* in the Council of Trent, July 16, 1562. "...*teaches and declares that the laity and clerics who are not celebrating are not bound by any divine command to receive the Sacrament of the Eucharist under both species.*"[47]

---

[42]Council of Trent DS 1642
[43]#1378
[44]#1378, #1379, and #1380
[45]Greek rooted Latin word
[46]#1390
[47]Chapter 1 - decree on Communion under both Species

"...this holy Council declares that it must be professed that the whole and entire Christ and the true Sacrament is received even under one species alone, and therefore, as far as the benefits concerned, those who receive only one species are not deprived of any grace necessary for salvation."[48]

But it quotes the General Instructions of the Roman Missal (549) which states that *"the sign of Communion is more complete when given under both kinds, since in that form the sign of the Eucharistic meal appears more clearly."*

Those Catholic brothers and sisters in Christ who have the use of reason must receive Holy Communion once during the year, preferably during the Easter season. However, the Church teaches that Communion should be received every time we take part in the Mass, at least weekly, and if possible, daily.

The effects of Holy Communion are the remission of sin, union with Christ and increase of grace, remission of venial sins and temporal punishment, preservation from mortal sin, perseverance in good and a pledge of eternal life.

†††

As you can tell from the above and from our books and television programs on the Holy Eucharist, we have a great love for Jesus in His Real Presence. When did it start, this love affair we have with the Eucharist?

Penny's reflection:

I never knew Him with my head until I was 46 years old. I had left Jesus and His Church because I did not know Him in the Eucharist. I cannot remember a day I have not loved Jesus. Even when I was crying out, in anger, through hurt, believing He had betrayed me by taking my son, I know now I never stopped loving Him.

I didn't know much about the teachings of the Church, growing up. Oh, we children went to church every Sunday

---

[48]Chapter 3 - decree on Communion under both Species

with Daddy while Mama cooked. And if we were not in an area where there was a Catholic Church, Daddy brought us to another church, it didn't matter what denomination. We were very *ecumenical* before I ever heard the expression.

Now, remember I did not know that Jesus was present in the Eucharist - Body, Blood, Soul and Divinity. But when we would leave one of the non-Catholic churches Daddy took me to, I would comment, "*I don't feel Jesus in there, the way I do in St. Joseph's Church back home.*" [This is in no way suggesting that Jesus is not present in the assembly of believers in churches ("*...where two or more are gathered in My Name...*"[49]) outside of the Catholic Church; I simply did not feel Him, except in our Catholic Church.] My father would insist He was there; I just had to look around at all the loving faces around me in church to see He was in their midst. But I did not feel Jesus there. Was I like the men on the road to Emmaus? Did I too, only recognize Him in the Eucharist during the Sacrifice of the Mass (the breaking of the Bread)?

I remember how Bob tried to keep me a child; he liked the simple child-like faith I had in the Lord. But the problem was that it was not child-like but childish! One thing I do remember, is how I would suddenly feel at the time of consecration, without knowing with my head what was happening. I would suddenly feel tears coming to my eyes and an excitement I could not explain. Oh, sweet Jesus, it was You all the time, reaching out to me, calling me by name.

I had a heart knowledge of Jesus; I loved Him the way a teen-ager loves, but it was not enough. When the going got rough because I did not have a synthesis - head and heart knowledge, I left Him and His Church. But He never left me. I know now that He had the Hounds of Heaven always there with me, biting at my heels, pulling me back to Him.

---

[49]Mt 18:20

I wounded Jesus when I left Him, and I will never stop grieving over that. But when He took over in my life and opened my eyes as well as my heart to His Presence in my life, how much He loved me, the price He paid for me on the Cross, then I really knew how much I loved Him, and no matter what happens, I can never deny Jesus again.

This is why we have to reach out to you who are in the Church. Learn about your Faith, so you will never fall victim to the evil one who is waiting in the shadows, ready to lead you like the Judas goat, to your destruction. There is a saying among sheepherders that no sheep will lead other sheep to slaughter. They place a goat (called a "*Judas goat*") in the pen and it is this *Judas goat*, they follow to their death.

And to you, who do not know why you are no longer Catholic (as up to the 16th Century we were all Catholic with the exception of the Greek and Russian Orthodox), please learn about the Faith of your ancestors, the Church founded by Christ Himself. There is so much to learn about the Eucharist, even this chapter just touches on the fringes of this great Sacrament. Read our two books on the Miracles of the Eucharist. Read the Instructions in the Roman Missal. Get the Catechism of the Catholic Church if you don't already have one. And if you have one, open it up and read it. Get it earmarked and dirty. Coffee stains on the cover is not a shame. Highlight it. Make references that you can retrieve easily. Remember, the Eucharist is the Source and Summit of Christian life. *It doesn't get better than that!*

Our Church is like the Hope Diamond, a perfect stone carved by the *Arch Diamond Cutter*. We call her Mother Church. Her light comes from Jesus Christ Who dwells within, her haunting melody from the Angels who adore Jesus on the Altar, her compassionate love from Mother Mary who never left the foot of the Cross and is Mother of the Church, her flawless wisdom from the Holy Spirit, the Paraclete, Who guides her, her wisdom from the Father Who had her in His Mind and Heart at the beginning of the world.

As the Hope Diamond came from man piercing the surface of the earth, our Church flowed from the Heart of Jesus that was pierced out of love for man. The Hope Diamond is priceless; the Church is beyond cost, bought by the Blood of the Lamb. And we love her so. She is our life. The Church and Jesus are one. As where you find Jesus, you will find Mary, so likewise, wherever you find the Church you will find Jesus. Come Home, all you who are weary. Jesus is waiting for you. His burden is light and the joy you will know is beyond anything you have ever known in your life. I guarantee it!

Oh Sacrament Most Holy
Oh Sacrament Divine
All Praise and All Thanksgiving
Be every moment Thine.
We adore the Wounds on Thy Sacred Head
with sorrow, deep and true;
may every thought of ours today
be an act of love for You.
We adore the Wounds in Thy Sacred Hands
with sorrow, deep and true;
may every work of our hands today
be an act of love for You.
We adore the Wounds in Thy Sacred Feet
with sorrow, deep and true;
may every step we take today
be an act of love for You.
We adore the Wounds of Thy Sacred Heart
with sorrow, deep and true;
may every beat of our hearts today
be an act of love for You.
Oh Sacrament Most Holy,
Oh Sacrament Divine
All Praise and all Thansksgiving
be every moment Thine.

Whose sins you shall forgive...
The Sacrament of Penance

Padre Pio spent hours each day in the Confessional,
hearing the confessions of people from all over the world

God being God is love, never changing, and His love, like Him in never changing, always there - even when we sin. God to remain God must love us, for He is Love. But we do not have to love Him to remain who we are. It makes you want to cry when you think of such a one-sided relationship.

"If we say we have no sin in us,
we are deceiving ourselves
and refusing to admit the truth;

but if we acknowledge our sins,
then God who is faithful and just
will forgive our sins and purify us
from everything that is wrong.
To say that we have never sinned
is to call God a liar
and to show that His word is not in us.[1]

"I am writing this, my children,
to stop you sinning;
but if anyone should sin,
we have our advocate with the Father,
Jesus Christ, who is just;
He is the sacrifice that takes our sins away,
and not only ours,
but the whole world's."[2]

Ours is a God we can count on. He knows our weakness, our human nature. When we sin, we break relationship with God; He continues to love us. He does not break relationship with us. He gives us a way to relieve ourselves of our guilt and be reconciled with Him and the Church.

Your sins are forgiven...

Those He commissioned, Peter and his successors - His *Ambassadors of Christ* of the last 2000 years, He gave the power to forgive men their sins and through this forgiveness turn their souls toward conversion.

Jesus asked the Father from the Cross to *"forgive them; they know not what they do."*[3] But man's garments, first made clean by the Blood of the Lamb, become soiled by sin. Knowing His children's frailty, Christ left this ministry of forgiveness and reconciliation to His priests; through them

---

[1] 1Jn 1:8-10
[2] 1Jn 2:1-2
[3] Lk 23:23

He hears and absolves man of his sins so that once again he is washed clean.

The Church teaching on the Sacrament of Penance, also called the Rite of Reconciliation is fairly simple and straightforward. It is as follows:

When a person sins, God, in His unconditional love, gives His children a way to reconcile, to renew the relationship, and that is by confessing the sins. There are three necessary things for a good confession:

Contrite Heart - Sincere sorrow for the sins committed and a firm purpose to not sin again.

Real or Physical Confession - The sinner confesses to an ordained priest all the sins he/she remembers.

Penance - the penance is decided by the priest-confessor, based on the severity of the sins. Usually, penance consists of prayers, fasting or almsgiving, but there are situations where restitution may be required, as in the case of stealing. This is up to the priest to decide.

The mandate to forgive sins was given to the Apostles by Jesus.[4] But in the early Church, going to confession was more difficult than we experience today. The penitent made a private and individual confession to a bishop, and the penance was made public. Serious sinners, those found guilty of murder, apostasy and fornication were put into the Order of Penitents, and made to wear sackcloth and ashes. They were not allowed to receive Holy Communion until Holy Thursday of the year of their penance.

In Ireland, monks began hearing individual confessions much along the lines of what we do today. The sinner confessed privately; penance was private and milder, and absolution immediate. The penitent was allowed to take part in Holy Communion after absolution. Also the penitent was encouraged to confess sins other than those of a grave

---

[4]Mt 16:19 and Jn 20:23

or serious nature, or what we call venial sins (disobedience to God involving light moral matter or done without adequate knowledge, freedom and full consent).

And so, we confess to a priest!

The Catechism of the Catholic Church clearly states that: "*Confession to a priest is an essential part of the Sacrament of Penance.*" A penitent, after carefully examining his conscience for all his mortal and venial sins, must then confess them to a priest with faculties[5] to administer the Sacrament of Penance. In so doing, the penitent is really placing all his sins before the *Lord* for His Divine Mercy. Those who do not accept this gift left by Jesus Himself and refuse to do so, place nothing before the Lord, in His infinite Divine mercy, to forgive. Even sins that are secret are to be confessed. They are usually the ones that wound the Father the most. Jesus, through His priest, desires to *heal* the penitent. How can Jesus the Healer, through the priest's mediation *(in persona Christi* in the physical personhood of Jesus) administer the proper medicine (penance) if the wounds of sin are not exposed? "*the medicine cannot heal what it does not know.*"[6]

Where does the priest get his authority?

Where in Holy Scripture does it say that we are to confess to a priest? is often the question demanded by non-Catholics. We turn to St. Paul's letter to the Corinthians:

"*...if anyone is in Christ, he is a new creation. The old world has passed away; now all is new. All this has been done by God, Who has reconciled us to Himself through Christ and **has given us the ministry of reconciliation.** I mean that God, in Christ, was reconciling the world to*

---

[5]Canonical faculties: authorization granted by the Holy See, a Bishop or Prelate, which enable the priest to act validly and licitly. Catholic Encyclopedia - Broderick

[6]Catechism of the Catholic Church #1456

Himself, not counting men's transgressions against them, and that **He has entrusted the message of reconciliation to us.** *This makes us ambassadors of Christ, God as it were appealing through us. We implore you, in Christ's Name: be reconciled to God!"[7]*

Christ left this mission to His apostles and to those whom they would ordain. He had risen from the dead. He had appeared to Mary Magdalen. Afraid of the Jews, the Apostles were locked away in the Upper Room. Jesus appeared to them (although the doors were locked) and said *"Peace be with you."* Then Jesus breathed on them and said:

"Receive the Holy Spirit.
If you forgive men's sins,
they are forgiven them;
if you hold them bound,
they are held bound."[8]

Upon rising from the dead, one of Christ's first acts was to commission His disciples to forgive men's sins, and those disciples (His bishops and priests) who would follow to do likewise! We read in the Catechism of the Catholic Church:

"Since Christ entrusted to His apostles the ministry of reconciliation, bishops who are their successors, and priests, the bishops' collaborators, continue to exercise this ministry. Indeed bishops and priests, by virtue of Holy Orders[9] have the power to forgive all sins in the Name of the Father, and of the Son and of the Holy Spirit."[10]

Throughout the centuries, there have been subtle changes in the Sacrament of Penance, but mostly in the accidental, or exterior aspects of the Sacrament. However, with the arrival of the major heresies leading up to and including the attack by Martin Luther and John Calvin, this

---

[7]2Cor 5:17-21
[8]Jn 20:21-24
[9]Read about this Sacrament in another chapter
[10]Catechism of the Catholic Church #1461

Sacrament came under particular attack, not only in its exterior forms, but in its validity.

Luther attacked the Church with such force, it became necessary for the Council of Trent to address all the issues brought against the Church by Luther with regard to *Penance.*

The Council of Trent, under the inspiration of the Holy Spirit, issued a doctrine on the Sacrament of Penance that was extremely vivid in all that it covered. It did not take anything for granted and, as far as was possible, encompassed every aspect possible. The titles of the various chapters of the Doctrine:

1. The Necessity and the Institution of the Sacrament of Penance.
2. The Difference Between the Sacraments of Penance and Baptism.
3. The Parts and the Effect of Penance
4. Contrition
5. Confession
6. The Minister of the Sacrament
7, Christian Marriages
8. The Reservation of Cases
9. The Necessity and Benefit of Satisfaction
10. Expiatory Works

In addition to these chapters, the Council issued fifteen canons confirming the Sacrament of Penance.

What are Indulgences?

"Indulgences have a direct correlation with Penance. We believe that sins are forgiven through the Sacrament of Penance. Indulgences do not forgive sins, but remit temporal punishment due to sins. Thus the Church's power of binding and loosing is exercised not only in the Sacrament of Penance but also in the granting of indulgences. For this reason, and because indulgences as granted in the Church today are historically the outgrowth of the practice of remitting a part or the whole of a Sacramental penance, the Church's pronouncements on indulgences are joined with those on the Sacrament of Penance.

"The Sacrament of Penance does not usually remove all temporal punishment to which the sinner is liable for his mortal or venial sins. This temporal punishment is usually suffered in Purgatory. This is why we pray for the souls in Purgatory, to remove some of their time, suffering for the remission of temporal punishment.

"The Church also grants indulgences for the remission of temporal punishment. Indulgences are granted under certain conditions such as the performance of good works, or the recitation of specified prayers. Three truths form the doctrinal basis for the practice of indulgences.

1.   The Church has the power of binding and loosing, conferred on it by Christ.[11]

2.   The satisfactory value of the works of Christ and the Saints forms a superabundant treasury.

3.   The Communion of Saints in Christ makes it possible for the Church to apply this treasury to the faithful, both living and dead."[12]

We take pilgrimages to Europe every year. In each of our pilgrimages, we visit certain shrines which offer Plenary Indulgences, *under the usual conditions*.

The usual conditions are:

1.   Confession and Communion within 8 days of having visited the shrine. This fulfills the requirement of being free from mortal or venial sin.

2.   Recitation of *at least* the Our Father, Hail Mary and Glory Be for the Holy Father's intention.

---

[11]Mt 16:19-18:18
[12]Catechism of the Catholic Church #1471

Plenary Indulgences can only be received once a day. Partial indulgences may be received many times per day, based on saying the prayers or doing whatever the requirements might be to be granted an indulgence.

An Indulgence can only be received by the person asking for it, or for the souls in Purgatory. We have a philosophy. If we ask for a Plenary indulgence for ourselves, we will be freed of any temporal punishment due for our sins which have been forgiven up until the moment we ask for them. But if you look at the Scripture passage at the beginning of this chapter from 1 John, you know that we're going to sin again pretty soon after.

However, if we offer that Plenary indulgence up for the Souls in Purgatory, we know that a soul will be released as soon as that Plenary indulgence is granted. That means that you have a soul in Heaven praying for you every time you release a soul from Purgatory by offering a Plenary indulgence.

†††

By our Baptism, we were cleansed of *Original Sin*.[13] But afterward, we sadly say *Yes* to the fallen angels and their temptations and fall into *Actual Sin*.[14] We have heard our priests say that they get all their reading done in the

---

[13]Original Sin - the sin we inherited from our first parents: Adam and Eve; more in chapter on Baptism.

[14]Actual Sin - a personal act that is *morally bad*, or the omission of some obliged good. (Catholic Encyclopedia-Broderick) [In the Confiteor during Holy Mass, we say "*I confess to Almighty God and to you, my brothers and sisters ... in what I have done and what I have failed to do....*"]

According to the manner of their commission, such sins may be interior or exterior; committed against God, one's neighbor, or one's self, according to their object; in gravity, either mortal or venial; from their cause, either committed in ignorance, weakness, or malice; and capital or noncapital with regard to whether they do or do not give rise to other sins. (Catholic Encyclopedia-Broderick)

confessional waiting for penitents who do not show up. Either our churches are filled with Saints, those already made perfect while still on earth, or we have the reception of many sacrilegious Communions every Sunday. Do we know with our heads and our hearts Who it is we are receiving? Do we know what happens during the Mass? If we do and do not go to confession, we risk condemnation. As St. Paul wrote: "*...whoever eats the bread or drinks the cup of the Lord unworthily sins against the Body and Blood of the Lord.*"[15]

Before we go to receive Our Lord in the Eucharist, if we truly believe that Our Lord is present in the Eucharist and we have the stain of mortal sin on our souls, we will desire not to *first* go but to first *run* to confession, to be absolved of these wounds against God; for every sin is wounding to God; every sin caused Jesus pain in the Garden of Gethsemane, on the Way to the Cross and on the Cross those excruciating last three hours of His Life. Once having confessed to a priest, been absolved of all our sins and having fulfilled our penance, a wave of freedom flows over us, and we are anxious to enter into that union, that *Communion* with the Lord Who awaits us.

As you hear the priest intone this prayer of absolution, close your eyes and see Jesus before you speaking, forgiving, welcoming you to full life with Him and the Father:

"*God the Father of mercies,*
through the death and the resurrection of His Son
has reconciled the world to Himself
and sent the Holy Spirit among us
for the forgiveness of sins;
through the ministry of the Church
may God give you pardon and peace,
and I absolve you from your sins

---

[15] 1Cor 11:27

in the Name of the Father, and of the Son, and of the Holy Spirit."[16]

I have never gotten over those words of consolation, our priest intones at the end of my confession. Suddenly, I feel a great weight lifted from my soul; I feel light, like I could fly. I find myself with a joy mingled with tears: *"He loves me; my Lord loves me!"* I want to shout to the world. Instead, I kneel in adoration, say my penance and leave the church with my family. I feel great!

I remember one day, overhearing my grandson and a non-Catholic sharing about confession. His friend said he went directly to Jesus and asked *Him* for forgiveness. Then I heard my boy say: *"Yes, but I have need to hear the words "You are forgiven!"*

In our talks at the various conferences around the country, we share about the psychological benefits of Confession. There was a survey taken by the American Society of Psychiatrists. Before World War II, Catholics numbered only about 10% of therapists' patients. They went to their priest who forgave them their sins in the name of Jesus. He gave them absolution. He told them they were forgiven.

Today, Catholics represent somewhere about 40% of therapists' patients. In the survey done, it was determined that before a Catholic patient developed the same trust level with his therapist as he had with a priest he had never met before the first time he walked into a Confessional, was approximately 4 visits. We have the gift of Reconciliation. All we had to do is accept it.

The Sacrament of Healing

When we are baptized *"man receives new life in Christ."[17]* Now the world cannot see this life, as we carry it in *vessels*

---

[16]formula of absolution - Catechism #1449
[17]Catechism of the Catholic Church #1420

molded by the Potter from the finest clay. These *vessels*, which we call our bodies, are, although forgiven of Original Sin by Baptism[18] *"subject to suffering, illness, and death."*[19] With Baptism, we shed the sins of our first parents Adam and Eve and are given a new life, new beginnings in and with God but this new life can be weakened and crippled and *"even lost by sin."*[20]

I think of the many times now, as when Jesus walked the earth, the sick and infirmed do not know what they really need, is to hear that their sins are forgiven. Jesus first said to the paralytic, *"My child, your sins are forgiven."* Then to prove to the scribes, whom He knew were thinking He was blaspheming, He said: *"...to prove to you that the Son of Man has authority on earth to forgive sins, I order you: pick up your stretcher and go off home."*[21] Our Lord healed, giving sight to the blind, and restoring new freedom to the lame, but He knew that the greatest healing that had to come about was not that of the body but of the soul. Jesus wanted to continue healing, even after He rose from the dead and ascended to Heaven. He willed that His Church, through the guidance and power of the Holy Spirit, continue this Sacrament of *"healing and salvation."*[22]

"Those who approach the Sacrament of Penance obtain pardon from the Mercy of God for the offense committed against Him, and are, at the same time, reconciled with the Church which they have wounded by their sins and which by charity, by example, and by prayer labors for their conversion."[23]

---

[18]see chapter on Sacrament of Baptism
[19]Catechism of the Catholic Church #1420
[20]Catechism of the Catholic Church #1420
[21]Mk 2:9-12
[22]Catechism of the Catholic Church #1421
[23]Lumen Gentium 11, Par 2

It is called the *Sacrament of Conversion* in that it makes Sacramentally present Jesus' call to conversion, the first step in returning to the Father from whom we have strayed.

It is called the Sacrament of Penance since it consecrates the sinner's personal and ecclesial steps of conversion and satisfaction.

It is called the *Sacrament of Confession* since the confessing of sins to a priest is an essential part of the Sacrament. It is also a confession of acknowledgement and praise of God's Holiness and His Mercy towards sinful man.

It is called the *Sacrament of Forgiveness* since through the words of the priest, God grants the penitent "pardon and peace."

It is called the *Sacrament of Reconciliation* because it reconciles the sinner to the Church.

The Eucharist leads us to the Sacrament of Reconciliation

The *Sacrament of Penance* leads us to the *Sacrament of the Eucharist*. But an usual thing happens every time, we give Retreats or Days of Recollection, especially when speaking on the Miracles of the Eucharist. We notice more and more people lining up to go to *confession*! As they became more and more aware of the *Real Presence* of Jesus in their midst in the Eucharist, in His Body, Blood, Soul and Divinity, how He comes to them during the Mass, how He remains with them in our Church in the Tabernacle, or exposed in a Monstrance for Eucharistic Adoration, changes come about, a metanoia (a conversion), they begin to understand the magnitude of Jesus' love for them, and their hearts long to receive absolution of their sins so that they can welcome the Bridegroom into a spotless dwelling.

During our talks, it comes to them, through God's generous love bringing about the Miracles of the Eucharist (to prove He is *truly* with us), that the Mass is first a *Sacrifice* and then because of that *Sacrifice* it is a *Celebration*, their lives take on a different dimension. They become a people truly consecrated to the Lord and His Church, and the light that emanates from their eyes, eyes cleared by confession and illuminated by the Eucharist, send beams of Christ's Love to all they encounter, and through that light, evangelization comes about.

Souls freed from sin become souls open *to be loved* by the Father and *to love* their brothers and sisters. As each soul becomes filled with head and heart knowledge of the Lord, of what is really going to happen on the Altar during the Consecration of the Mass, it longs to become a bride like the five in Holy Scripture who prepared their oil and lamps for when the bridegroom would come.[24]

I equate going to confession to expecting an important guest, a priest or bishop, a religious like Mother Angelica; we find ourselves cleaning our home spotlessly; and then that accomplished, laboring over a hot stove preparing our choicest dishes, the aroma of fresh bread filling the house. There is an excitement, as we set the table with our finest china, silver and stemware on our best tablecloth. Flowers are carefully chosen. New unused candles are placed in their holders. Not only is our home in readiness, but we keep changing our clothes until we have decided what we will wear for this special guest.

I look upon going to confession as relationship with Jesus - *How much do I love Him? What am I willing to do to grow closer to Him?* Preparing to go to confession, I find myself thinking of my union with Him in the Eucharist that will come about when I receive Him in Holy Communion during Mass. Then my heart and mind travel to that day when I will behold His Beatific Vision in Heaven, and I cannot describe the emotions that run through me; Jesus is waiting for me on the Altar. Suddenly, I feel young again. I

---

[24]Mt 25:1-13

want to be the best for Him, as I did for my spouse the day we were married. The excitement I felt when I was about to be joined to my spouse in Holy Matrimony fills me now even more deeply.

I can still remember the day we were married in the Church. Before receiving the Sacrament of Matrimony, this Holy Sacrament that would make God one with us, we first went to our confessor to receive the Sacrament of Penance. We wanted to tear down any old walls that could separate us from one another. We wanted nothing of the past to stand between us. We individually knelt before him asking forgiveness for that which we had done and that which we had failed to do. When the priest intoned the final blessing, invoking the Holy Spirit, absolving us in the *Name of the Father, and of the Son and and of the Holy Spirit*, all our yesterdays, filled with remorse, passed away. We were a new creation, because our priest, standing in for Jesus, wiped away all our tears and fears. We were alive; it was a new day; a new life was to begin and we knew the peace of that moment and the joy that was to come. We were ready to make a commitment to each other, and a lifetime covenant with Jesus. The light of a new life was about to begin and there was no fog of unresolved sins to block out the Son. We could look at each other and see Jesus in one another.

I do not look forward to going to confession at times, I am ashamed to admit. But after having gone to confession and having heard those precious words of forgiveness, I suddenly feel tears come to my eyes, those of awe and wonder at this loving, generous God Who loves us so much He left this means of consolation through forgiveness to us, His children.

Thank You Jesus; thank You Father; thank You Holy Spirit for loving us so much. Let us spend eternity with you.

"Is anyone among you sick?...."

The Sacrament of the Anointing of the Sick

"Is anyone among you sick? He should summon the presbyters of the Church, and they should pray over him and anoint him with oil in the name of the Lord, and the prayer of faith will save the sick person, and the Lord will raise him up."[1]

All the Sacraments are important; all are special gifts from the Lord to those who love Him.[2] But this Sacrament could very easily be called the Sacrament of *"The Lord takes care of His own."* For anyone who has ever had the feeling that they are alone in the world, that the Lord just left them here and went off somewhere, that He's only interested in catching us in some terrible sin so He can cast us into the fires of hell, read and understand how much the Lord really loves you, learn about this awesome Sacrament, the last Sacrament of the Church.

Union with the Passion of Christ - By the grace of this Sacrament, the sick receive the strength and gift of uniting themselves more closely to Christ's Passion: in a certain way *they are consecrated* to bear fruit by becoming one with the Savior through His redemptive Passion. Suffering, a consequence of original sin, acquires a new meaning; it becomes a participation in the saving work of Jesus.[3]

Redemptive suffering: For people who are suffering, especially in the throes of death, but any type of suffering, whatever the pain, *it does not have to go to waste!* As with Jesus' suffering before them it can be offered to the Father for the conversion and redemption of the world.

This is why we have such a problem with Jack Kervorkian and any who would assist suicide or contemplate suicide. They are robbing themselves and those whom they

---

[1]Jas 5:14-15
[2]*cf* Jas 1:12
[3]*cf* Catechism of the Catholic Church #1521

assist, of a very special grace, a power that no one has except those who suffer, and use that suffering for others.

†The suffering can be offered up for the Souls in Purgatory;
†it can be offered up for the conversion of sinners;
†it can be offered up for spouses who have separated;
†it can be offered up for a child who has left the church,
†it can be offered up for runaways, drug addicts, alcoholics.
Leave them alone, Jack Kervorkian! *Don't take that power away from the people of God!*

The Anointing of the sick is a true Sacrament instituted by Christ and promulgated by St. James, whose matter is anointing with oil and whose form is in certain words.

The Minister must be a priest or a bishop. The oil is usually that which has been blessed on Holy Thursday at the Chrism Mass at the Diocesan Cathedral. However, in the event that is not possible, the priest administering the Sacrament may bless the oil, himself.

The first grace of the Sacrament is one of *strengthening, peace* and *courage* to overcome the difficulties that go with the condition of serious illness or the frailty of old age. This grace is a gift of the Holy Spirit, Who renews trust and faith in God and strengthens against the temptations of the evil one, the temptation to discouragement and anguish in the face of death. This assistance from the Lord by the power of the Spirit is meant to lead the sick person to healing of the soul, but also of the body if such is God's Will. Furthermore, *"if he has committed sins, he will be forgiven."*[4]

Additional benefits of this Sacrament are
†grace from the Holy Spirit
†remission of sins[5]

---

[4]Jas 5:15 - *cf* Council of Trent (1551)DS 1717

[5]If circumstances prevented the dying person from confessing before the priest administered the Sacrament, even mortal sin would be forgiven through this Sacrament. *(The Church Teaches - Jesuit Fathers of St. Mary's College - St. Marys, KS - Pg 322)*

†spiritual healing
†arousing trust in the divine mercy
†comforting of the soul
†removal of the effects of sins
†strength against temptations of the devil
†and sometimes health for the body.

In addition, the Church makes available to those who are about to die, the Eucharist as *Viaticum*. *"The celebration of the Eucharist as Viaticum, food for the passage through death to eternal life, is the Sacrament proper to the dying Christian."*[6]

"Thus, just as the Sacraments of Baptism, Confirmation and the Eucharist form a unity called *'The Sacraments of Christian Initiation,'* so too it can be said that Penance, the Anointing of the Sick and the Eucharist as Viaticum constitute at *the end of Christian life,* 'the Sacraments that prepare for our Heavenly homeland' or the Sacraments that complete the earthly pilgrimage."[7]

They say that the Catholic Religion is a hard one to live by, but an easy one to die by. At the hour of death, this Sacrament of the Church, the Anointing of the Sick, but also called *Sacramentum exeuntium* (the Sacrament of those departing life),[8] is given to all who are at the point of death. It is the last anointing of the Church. *"It completes the holy anointings that mark the whole Christian life: that of Baptism which sealed the new life in us, and that of Confirmation which strengthened us for the combat of this life."*[9]

---

[6]Roman Missal #175-211
[7]Catechism of the Catholic Church #1525
[8]Council of Trent #1551
[9]Catechism of the Catholic Church #1523

Above: ***Jesus performed His first Public Miracle in honor of the Sacrament of Marriage-Feast of Cana.***

Above: ***Church of Cana***

"...and the two shall become one"

The Sacrament of Matrimony

This chapter is very close to our hearts as we believe firmly in the Sacrament of Matrimony. We have always served the Lord as a married couple. Even in the early 80's when many of our friends were entering into the Diaconate program in Los Angeles, we felt we could better serve the Lord through our Sacrament. We believe that we have "couple power," a term which was given to us on our Marriage Encounter Weekend in May, 1975, a weekend which changed our lives. Nothing that ever had been before, was ever the same or ever would be. We truly believe that we were empowered by the Holy Spirit on that weekend.

Marriage has always played an important part in Salvation History. The Catechism of the Catholic Church tells us "Sacred Scripture begins with the creation of man and woman in the image and likeness of God and concludes with a vision of 'the Wedding Feast of the Lamb.'"

"So the Lord God cast a deep sleep on the man, and while he was asleep, He took out one of his ribs and closed up its place with flesh. The Lord God then built up into a woman the rib that He had taken from the man. When He brought her to the man, the man said:

'This one, at last, is bone of my bones
and flesh of my flesh;
This one shall be called woman
for out of 'her man' this one has been taken.'

That is why a man leaves his father and mother and clings to his wife, and the two of them become one flesh."[1]

Then again at the end of Scripture in the Book of Revelation:

"Let us rejoice and be glad and give Him glory.
For the wedding day of the Lamb has come,

---

[1]Gen 2:21-24

His bride has made herself ready."[2]
and then again:

"Then the Angel said to me: 'Write this: Blessed are those who have been called to the wedding feast of the Lamb.'

"And he said to me, 'These words are true; they come from God."[3]

It goes on to say that Scripture speaks throughout of Marriage and its "mystery,"[4] its institution and the meaning God has given it, its origin and its end, its various realizations throughout the history of salvation, the difficulties arising from sin and its renewal "in the Lord" in the New Covenant of Christ and the Church.[5]

In the introduction to the Sacraments, we spoke of how the Sacraments of Holy Orders and Matrimony have been grouped together as specially Consecrated Sacraments. Holy Orders was created by Jesus Christ Himself at the Last Supper. Matrimony was created by God the Father in the Garden of Eden at the very beginning of Salvation History. Marriage has played an important part down through the millenniums with regard to Salvation and Redemption.

From a very logical viewpoint, the Sacrament of Marriage, the couple joined to each other with God and the Church Community as witness, are what creates family. The Church depends on family for its very existence. The family of God builds the Church with its members, supports the Church with its time and talents, builds the buildings with its donations and ultimately feeds the ministries of the Church with its children, especially the priesthood. The Church depends on the family for its very survival.

†††

---

[2]Rev 19:7
[3]Rev 19:9
[4]Eph 5:32
[5]Catechism of the Catholic Church #1602

We have visited Our Lady of Knock, Ireland, many times, taken slides and made a television program. But one time we were preparing a talk in the days when we used slides to show the shrines. We were working in a hotel room in New Orleans, preparing for a week of talks on Miracles of the Eucharist and the Apparitions of Our Lady.

One of the problems with authenticating Our Lady's visit to Knock shrine was that she didn't speak. This is almost impossible for an Irishman to conceive, Bob being Irish. As we looked at the slides of Knock, we realized how powerful a shrine and apparition that was, and how much Our Lady really said, without saying anything.

The first slide showed an altar, with a Paschal Lamb standing on it, a cross in back of it, surrounded by Angels - the Eucharist, and the Mass. Our Lady was telling us to *defend the Eucharist*, which has always been in jeopardy. If you destroy the Eucharist, you destroy the Church.

The next image was St. John the Evangelist, dressed as a bishop, holding Holy Scriptures in his hand, opened to the Book of Revelation. *Defend the Word*, which in our time is in danger of being destroyed. Many factors in and out of the Church would love to change Scripture. But it's like a woolen sweater. If you pull one thread out of the sweater, it completely unravels, and all you have is a pile of wool. If you destroy the Word, you destroy the Church.

The last image was Our Lady and St. Joseph. On the day we had taken this slide at Knock Shrine, a woman had placed a little baby in a basket in front of Our Lady and St. Joseph, as she knelt to pray. The silent message *screamed* out at us: *Defend the Family,* which is and has always been in jeopardy. Because you see, if you destroy the *Eucharist*, you destroy the Church; if you destroy the *Word*, you destroy the Church; if you destroy the *family*, you destroy the Church; you destroy the world.

We are sure that during this period in Ireland, 1879, when Mother Mary appeared, the family was in great jeopardy. We know that they were being split up by the famines, what with young men going over to America to earn a living so they could send money back home to Ireland. The British knew that there was only two things that held the Irish together, their faith in God and their family. Oh and one more thing, *Holy Stubbornness!*

We have always felt that the message of Our Lady of Knock, Ireland in 1879 was more for our time than for theirs. Since the 60's, the family has been the target of Satan and his cohorts all over the world. Drugs separated children from their parents. Drugs killed our children. It's a fact that more young people die each year from drug overdoses than have died in the entire Viet Nam War.

Divorce separated and destroyed marriages and family. When divorce became legalized, and no fault divorce was adopted, first by California in 1968, and eventually by every state in the union, Marriage became an endangered species. To this day, the rate of divorce each year is higher than the rate of marriages.

Divorce, single parent households, abortion and now, same sex marriages are destroying the fiber of our family as we have known it. The enemy is doing a masterful job. He won't win, but he's giving us a run for our money. However, the Lord has given us a miracle which can turn all this around. It's up to us to use the miracle. It goes like this:

"There was an independent study done recently on marriage. The findings were as follows:

2 out of every 3 marriages end in divorce.

If the couple goes to the same church to worship once a week,

1 out of 50 marriages end in divorce.

If the couple prays together,

1 out of 150 marriages end in divorce.

If Jesus is the center of their marriage,

twenty four hours a day, seven days a week,
1 out of 1500 marriages end in divorce."[6]

††††

Marriage has been a key factor in the Church from Biblical times. St. Paul spent much time teaching his people,[7] especially those in Corinth about the necessity of Marriage, and a faithful Marriage at that. The Roman and Greek philosophies regarding Marriage and morals in Marriage were loose, to say the least. Asking new Christians (remember, Paul evangelized to the pagans or gentiles, who basically had no moral code) to follow a strict moral and fidelity code, was a very touchy proposition. Rome and Corinth of the middle first century was morally very much like the world of today - permissiveness and promiscuity were the code of behavior. While the Romans accepted the importance of Marriage, it was for different reasons; they were trying to maintain a political and patriarchal discipline.

Man and woman, joined together as husband and wife, have been part of God's plan from the very beginning. A beautiful reading, often used at weddings, is St. Paul's letter to the Ephesians,

"Give way to one another in obedience to Christ. Wives should regard their husbands as they regard the Lord, since as Christ is head of the Church and saves the whole body, so is a husband the head of the wife; and as the Church submits to Christ, so should wives to their husbands in everything. Husbands should love their wives just as Christ loved the Church and sacrificed Himself for her to make her holy.

"...In the same way, husbands must love their wives as they love their own bodies; for a man to love his wife is for him to love himself."[8]

---

[6]*We Came Back to Jesus* - Bob and Penny Lord 1988 - Pg 54
[7]1Cor 7:39 - Eph 5:31-32
[8]Eph 5:21-29

Jesus tells us:

"Have you not read that the Creator from the beginning made them male and female and that He said: *'This is why a man must leave father and mother, and cling to his wife, and the two become one body?'* They are no longer two, therefore, but one body. So then, what God has united, man must not divide."[9]

Also, although Marriage had been created by God the Father at the beginning of time with the mating of Adam and Eve, Jesus raised it to the level of a Sacrament with the Scripture passage above. Another thing that we'd like to mention while we're on the subject of Marriage is that Jesus performed His first Public Miracle in honor of the Sacrament of Marriage at the Wedding Feast of Cana.

In the early days of our Pilgrimage Ministry, we brought pilgrims to the Holy Land four and five times a year. Each of our pilgrimages included a trip to the little Church of Cana which was built over the place where Jesus' Miracle of turning water into wine took place. There was a special service available to married couples at that church. Our priest led all the married couples, as we recommitted our vows of Marriage. This was a very special time for us. It brought back to us the importance and dedication we had to our Sacrament.

The Catechism of the Catholic Church also affirms that Jesus has raised the institution of Marriage to Sacramental form.

"The matrimonial covenant, by which a man and a woman establish between themselves a partnership of the whole of life, is by its nature ordered toward the good of the spouses and the procreation and education of

---

[9]Mt 19:5-6

offspring; this covenant between baptized persons has been raised by Christ to the dignity of a Sacrament."[10]

There are a few things in that statement which need our attention. One is "covenant" as opposed to "contract." Covenant means a relationship that recognizes spiritual equality of the spouses and their capacity to enter into an agreement which demands a gift of the whole person, one to another. Once this covenant begins, the spouses are joined by the unique bond of marriage. If both are baptized, by the very fact that consent is expressed, the Sacrament of Marriage is received. The priest is not the minister in the Sacrament; the couple is. The priest represents the community of the Church as an official witness.

Legally and canonically, if two free and capable, baptized Catholics exchange marital consent according to canonical form, the law presumes that the consent is valid and that a Sacrament has come into existence. The law does not say the spouses must have faith, yet the theological sources, including Vatican II, state clearly that the Sacraments *presuppose* and *require* faith.

"The parties to a Marriage covenant are a baptized man and woman, *free* to contract Marriage, who *freely* express their consent; "to be free" means:
-    not being under constraint;
-    not impeded by any natural or ecclesiastical law.[11]

The Church holds the exchange of consent between the spouses to be the *indispensable element* that "makes the marriage."[12] If consent is lacking, there is no marriage.

The consent consists in a "human act by which the partners mutually give themselves to each other." "I take you to be my wife." - "I take you to be my husband." This consent

---

[10]Catechism of the Catholic Church #1601 - taken from Canon 1055, Par 1

[11]Catechism of the Catholic Church #1625

[12]Canon 1057, Par 1

that binds the spouses to each other finds its fulfillment in "the two becoming one flesh."

The consent must be an act of the will of each of the contracting parties, free of coercion or grave external fear.[13]

"For this reason (or for other reasons that render the Marriage null and void) the Church, after an examination of the situation by the competent ecclesiastical tribunal, can declare the nullity of a marriage, i.e. that the marriage never existed.[14] In this case the contracting parties are free to marry, provided the natural obligations of a previous union are discharged."[15]

The other crucial area of forming the bond of marriage is "Consummation of the Marriage bond," at which point the marriage becomes *indisolluble* in the eyes of the Church.

"Conjugal love involves a totality, in which all the elements of the person enter - appeal of the body and instinct, power of feeling and affectivity, aspiration of the spirit and of will. It aims at a deeply personal unity, a unity that, beyond union in one flesh, leads to forming one heart and soul; it demands *indissolubility* and *faithfulness* in definitive mutual giving; and it is open to fertility. In a word it is a question of the normal characteristics of all natural conjugal love, but with a new significance which not only purifies and strengthens them, but raises them to the extent of making them the expression of specifically Christian values."[16]

---

[13]Canon 1103 - "*A marriage is invalid if it is entered into, due to force or grave fear inflicted from outside the person, even when inflicted unintentionally, which is of such a type that the person is compelled to choose Matrimony in order to be freed from it.*"

[14]Canons 1095-1107

[15]Canon 1071

[16]*cfHumanae Vitae* - Catechism of the Catholic Church #1643

In the reference from which the above section was taken, *Familiaris consortio 13*, there is a beautiful writing by an early theologian and apologist, Tertullian:

"How can I ever express the happiness of the marriage that is joined together by the Church, strengthened by an offering, sealed by a blessing, announced by Angels and ratified by the Father?...How wonderful the bond between two believers, with a single hope, a single desire, a single observance, a single service! They are both brethren and both fellow-servants; there is no separation between them in spirit or flesh; in fact they are truly two in one flesh, and where the flesh is one, one is the spirit."

As you can see above, the Church has always been aware of the importance of the Sacrament of Matrimony. In researching the Code of Canon Law we were amazed at the findings there. In the Introduction to Canons 1055-1165 under the heading of "Title VII - Marriage" it states:

"More canons are devoted to Marriage in the Code of Canon Law than to any other single subject (110). This extensive concern for Marriage reflects the importance of this Sacrament in the life of the Church."

The Catechism of the Catholic Church devotes sixty five sections to the Sacrament of Marriage. Within those sections are brought in Canons from the Code of Canon Law, teachings from various Ecumenical Councils, in particular the Council of Trent and Vatican II, multiple Scripture passages affirming Marriage as a Sacrament, and teachings from various theologians throughout history, including St. Paul, St. Augustine, St. Thomas Aquinas, Tertullian and many others.

Some of these teachings are so beautiful and so stirring that we must include them. Take time to digest what the author is saying. Read them over a few times. The gifts we are given with regard to the sanctity of Marriage, and how much a part of God's plan our Sacrament is, will delight you.

"Spouses are therefore the permanent reminder to the Church of what happened on the Cross; they are for one another, and for the children, witnesses to the salvation in which the Sacrament makes them sharers. Of this salvation event Marriage, like every Sacrament, is a memorial, actuation and prophecy:

"As a *memorial*, the Sacrament gives them the grace and duty of commemorating the great works of God and of bearing witness to them before their children.

"As *actuation*, it gives them the grace and duty of putting into practice in the present, towards each other and their children, the demands of a love which forgives and redeems.

"As *prophecy*, it gives them the grace and duty of living and bearing witness to the hope of the future encounter with Christ.

"Like each of the seven Sacraments, so also marriage is a real symbol of the event of salvation, but in its own way. The spouses participate in it as spouses, together, as a couple, so that the first and immediate effects of marriage (*res et Sacramentum*) is not supernatural grace itself, but the Christian conjugal bond, a typically Christian communion of two persons because it represents the mystery of Christ's incarnation and the mystery of His covenant."[17]

†††

Because Marriage is so key to society, such a pivotal movement in the rise and fall of civilization and our Church, it has been under monumental attack from the very beginning, down through the centuries.

One of the greatest problems to Marriage as a Sacrament is physical attraction followed by lack of understanding and preparation on the part of the recipients.

---

[17]*Familiaris Consortio* 13

Most of us have been there. At the time of infatuation, the only religious symbol we attach to our relationship with our loved one is that of the Angel Cupid. We are working on one agenda, Romance, which has nothing to do with what we should be focusing on. I'd like to share with you where I was at mentally and emotionally at this most important juncture of my life. I'd like to share an excerpt from my life.

†††

"I was born with Irish Stubbornness. It can be converted into a virtue, they tell me, but I really don't believe my stubbornness has ever been used for anything but bullheadedness. When someone wants me to do something I don't want to do, or not do something I do want to do, I dig my heels into the ground like an Irish mule, and stand firm.

"This was my frame of mind when Penny and I sat before a chubby priest in northern New Jersey in December of 1958. She had been divorced and we were going to be married. At her request, we went to talk to the Catholic priest about being married in the Church. I knew there was no way. Her first marriage had been blessed in the Church, some 12 years after she had been married, in an effort to save the marriage. This priest had performed the marriage himself. He was not about to tell us it could be annulled. They didn't do things like that, not in 1958, anyway.

"I was calm, cordial, and respectful, although antagonistic and bored. We weren't doing anything wrong, and this whole interview was so much nonsense. My cordiality went out the window, when the priest told us we would be living in sin. I exploded. In my mind, I called him every hypocrite in the book. In actuality, I told him what Penny's and the childrens' lives had been like, not being able to practice their religion openly, being Catacomb Catholics. The marriage should never have been blessed in the Church in the first place, and he should not have done it. He knew Penny's first husband much better than I, and it had been obvious to me that he had no intention of fulfilling a Catholic marriage contract.

"How could this priest possibly say that by being married to me, where she and the children could practice their religion without any hindrance, was a sin; whereas being married to her first husband, a Jewish man, where religion was a constant obstacle and cause for major arguments, was not a sin. The priest told me it would be next to impossible to prove that her first husband had no intention of living up to the marriage contract he had made when they were married in the Church. But I wasn't listening. I was on a roll.

"I accused this priest, and the whole Catholic Church of condemning Penny and the children to a life of misery. I ended my tirade with "*If that's the stand the Catholic Church wants to take, then we don't want any part of it. We don't need the Catholic Church to worship God. We don't need any Church.*"[18]

"How foolish we are as children. How prone we are to make brash statements that we can't ever expect to live with. That day, in front of that priest, I truly believe that Jesus, Mary, all my friends, the Angels and Saints, were there, rooting for me, praying I wouldn't make a fool of myself. How they must have wept when I turned my back on them. I know for myself, no sooner had the words slipped out of my stubborn mouth, than I wished I had never said them. Tears welled up in my eyes; my tongue became thick. I couldn't talk. I told Penny I always got this way when I got angry. But truly, I was sorry for my big mouth. I wanted to cry. In my mind's eye, I could see my Heavenly Family, so sad, but mostly, my best friend Mary. I had betrayed her so cruelly. Could she ever forgive me? The Lord has forgiven me that

---

[18]By the grace of God, Penny did get an annulment. But you can read more about it in their story, *We Came Back to Jesus.*

brashness I had in my younger days. But He has never let me forget it."[19]

✝✝✝

I would like to think that the Bob and Penny of 1958 were an exception to the rule, as we thought we were, but unfortunately, we were just like any other young couple *in love.* Love conquers all. We didn't need a church; we had each other. What we didn't know, and what so many young people don't consider before Marriage, is that this is the most important thing you will ever do in your life. If we're going to enter into this Sacrament in a Sacramental way, we must know what we're doing. We must be prepared.

The Church has for too long presumed that the people who want to get married have the same goals as the Church. But we're finding that's not the case at all. We know that many Catholics, married in a Catholic church, go through the ceremony with little if any commitment to the obligations of a Catholic marriage.

Unfortunately, for countless people, the Sacrament of Marriage is just the ceremony part of a big wedding with bridesmaids and ushers, maid of honor and best man, rehearsals and rehearsal dinners, receptions where the bride and groom sincerely try to keep members of the various families who are not speaking to each other at arms length, and just as sincerely try to keep the reception list under 400.

The Church has insisted in recent years that couples considering the Sacrament of Marriage go through extensive Marriage preparation, whether it be an Engaged Encounter weekend, or Pre-Cana Conference, where couples force themselves into taking off the rose-colored glasses and look at their future lives together. Sometimes it works; sometimes it doesn't.

---

[19]*We Came Back to Jesus* - Bob and Penny Lord 1988 - Pgs 65-67

But with the statistics against the longevity of Marriage, it's more important than ever that we give ourselves the best possible chance of making a success out of our Marriage, out of our future lives together. The future of the Church and the future of the world depend on strong family units, which have their basis in strong marriages.

What we have given you here is just a smattering of all that there is about the Sacrament of Marriage. There are so many intricacies, marrying a baptized non-Catholic, marrying a non-baptized non-Catholic, divorce situations, annulments, it's no wonder that the Code of Canon Law gave more canons to Marriage than any other single subject. Learn about Marriage as the Church teaches. Read the *Catechism of the Catholic Church* and the *Code of Canon Law*. Get a *Companion to* the *Catechism of the Catholic Church*.

Get involved in our Church in every aspect. The Sacraments, especially the Sacrament of Marriage are extremely important to the existence of our Church. We need you to be part of this beautiful Church. *Jesus needs you!*

Holy Orders

in the Life of the Church

The priesthood and our priests have always held a special place in our hearts. They are the lifeblood of our Church. They bring us Jesus. But do we know in how many ways they bring us Jesus? They are truly *"in persona Christi,"* representatives of Christ; they are Christ on earth for us.

If we genuinely believe that our priests are our Christ on earth, and our suffering Christ at that,[1] we can understand why their lives and their vocations have been so in jeopardy down through the ages. We can understand why they have constantly been the center of attack. Through the hands of the priest, we have communion with our God in the Eucharist. They are the instrument the Lord uses to come to us in the way He promised, in a real way. Just picture the Consecration of the Mass. Our priest holds up the bread and wine. As he says the prayers of Consecration, envision Jesus coming through the priest, the victim-priest, into the bread which he holds in his consecrated hands. The bread is no longer bread; it is Jesus. In the same way, when he raises the chalice, Jesus enters into the cup and there is no longer wine; there is Jesus. Jesus can't come to us,[2] without the cooperation of the priest.

The Eucharist is the Heart of the Church
Without the Eucharist, there is no life in the Church.
Without the Mass, there is no Eucharist.
Without the priest, there is no Mass."

Without our priests, we are hopeless and helpless.

Our priests are truly *"in persona Christi,"* in the person of Christ. The mandate was given them many times by Our Lord throughout His public Ministry, as when He sent them out the first time to evangelize:

---

[1]Council of Trent
[2]in the Eucharist

"And He called to Him the twelve, and began to send them out two by two, and gave them authority over unclean spirits. He charged them to take nothing for their journey except a staff; no bread, no bag, no money in their belts; but to wear sandals and not put on two tunics. And He said to them, *'Where you enter a house, stay there until you leave that place. And if any place will not receive you and they refuse to hear you, when you leave, shake off the dust that is on your feet for a testimony against them.'*

"So they went out and preached that men should repent. And they cast out many demons, and anointed with oil many that were sick and healed them."[3]

In response to the call of Jesus to His disciples, one of the most famous Scripture Passages with regard to the Ministry of Healing and the Ministry of Reconciliation by the priests comes to us from the Apostle St. James:

"Is there anyone among you suffering? Let him pray. Is any cheerful? Let him sing praise. Is any among you sick? Let him call for the elders (priests) of the church, and let them pray over him, anointing him with oil in the name of the Lord; and the prayer of faith will heal the sick man, and the Lord will raise him up; and if he has committed sins, he will be forgiven.

"Therefore, confess your sins to one another, and pray for one another, that you may be healed."[4]

The Lord spoke to our priests in John's Gospel:

"As the Father has sent Me, so also I send you....Whose sins you shall forgive, they are forgiven them, and whose sins you shall retain, they are retained."[5]

But the prime mandate we believe is when Jesus actually ordained them at the Last Supper with His

---

[3]Mk 6:7-13
[4]Jas 5:13-16
[5]Jn 20:23

command, "*Do this in memory of Me.*"   The Church has always interpreted this as a command by Our Lord for them and their successors in the priesthood to offer His Sacrifice. The Council of Trent has interpreted the Last Supper as a Sacrificial Meal, as opposed to the Protestants' contention that it was merely a religious meal.[6]

The Council equated His words "*This is My Blood of the New Covenant which is being shed for many unto the remission of sins*"[7] to have an historical connection to a covenant made between God and the Jews in the Old Testament:

"And he (Moses) sent young men of the people of Israel, who offered burnt offerings and sacrificed peace offerings of oxen to the Lord. And Moses took half the blood and put it in basins, and half of the blood he threw against the altar. Then he took the book of the covenant, and read it in the hearing of the people; and they said, 'All that the Lord has spoken, we will do, and we will be obedient.' And Moses took the blood and threw it upon the people, and said, 'Behold the blood of the covenant which the Lord has made with you in accordance with all these words.'"[8]

Therefore, our Church teaches that the ministry Christ gave to the Apostles and their successors was one of sacrifice.   We teach that the priestly office has been entrusted in a special way to a particular group within the Church, and that the rite by which they are invested is a true Sacrament that confers a special power and grace to equip them for that ministry, which is both sacrificial and pastoral.

---

[6]As mentioned in the chapter on the Councils, the Council of Trent addressed itself almost exclusively to defending the Church against the attacks of Martin Luther by condemning the heresies put forth by Luther and defining the Truths of our Church.

[7]Mt 26:28

[8]Ex 24:5-8

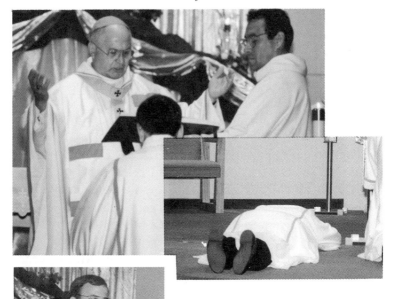

Sacrament of Holy Orders
Every Catholic should experience the
Ordination of a Priest.
We witnessed the Ordination of
Father Phil Henning of the
Arch-Diocese of San Antonio in
January 1994.

When you consider the priesthood of Padre Pio of Pietrelcina, who bore the wounds of Christ on his body for 50 years *in this century,* you have a perfect example of the priesthood being a ministry of Sacrifice. Padre Pio epitomized the expression "*victim priest*". Padre Pio lived to perform his priestly duties, in particular to offer the Sacrifice of the Mass.

As Padre Pio began vesting for Mass, his body began to bend forward. As he slowly approached the Altar, his body began to stoop over more and more as if he was being crushed under a heavy cross beam on his shoulders; his gait dragged, his face taking on the sorrow of His Lord and Savior. Color returned to his ashen face as he kissed the Altar. When he beat his breast during the Confiteor, it was as if he was accusing himself of all the sins committed by man. Huge tears flowed from his closed eyes onto his beard. The Gospel seemed to feed him as he contemplated on His Lord in His Word.

As the Mystery of the Sacrifice of the Mass unfolded, Padre Pio reached the pinnacle of suffering at the moment of Elevation of the host in Consecration. To quote a witness, "*In his eyes I read the expression of a mother who assists at the agony of her son on the scaffold, who sees him expire and who, choked with suffering, silently receives the bloodless body in her arms, able only to give slight caresses.*" Padre Pio shared willingly not only with Jesus in His Passion, but in that of His Mother.

Padre Pio was a willing prisoner of the Confessional, spending hours upon hours taking upon himself all the horrors of the sins being confessed by the thousands of penitents who came to him. Padre Pio "*knew everything and read in hearts the most intimate secrets.*" He always gave credit to God for the fatherly advise and compassion he had for those who sincerely came to him seeking reconciliation. He said, "*It is not I, but He who is in me and above me.*" But as he was gentle and encouraging to those who wished to change their life of sinfulness, he could be firm and almost brusque to those whom he *knew* were not truly sorry for the pain they were causing our Lord.

As our Lord Jesus was painfully struck in the Heart by the unfaithfulness of those of His Time, before and since, so our Lord chose to share that pain with Padre Pio. Not only did he have the Five Wounds of our Dear Lord, the Stigmata, but Padre Pio's heart was pierced as if by an arrow, *"I feel in the depths of my soul a wound that is always open and which causes me continual agony."*

Padre Pio had many gifts: bilocation, the Stigmata, perfect Confessor, the Essence of Heaven which flowed from his wounds to name a few, as well as the countless miracles attributed to him during his lifetime. But Padre Pio will not be Beatified and then later Canonized because of any of these signs of God's Favor, but because of his priestly faithfulness and obedience. As we pause in the choir loft where he so often prayed, and we kneel before the Crucifix where he received the Stigmata, Jesus' Words to Padre Pio become indelibly stamped on our hearts.

†

You call Me the Way	but you don't follow Me.
You call Me the Light	but you don't see Me.
You call Me the Teacher	but you don't listen to Me.
You call Me the Lord	but you don't serve Me.
You call Me the Truth	but you don't believe in Me.

Don't be surprised if one day, I don't know you!

†††

"Christ's work of redeeming mankind by His Sacrifice on the Cross presupposed His own Priesthood. This Priesthood Christ possessed in all its fullness by the very fact of His Incarnation, for the whole meaning of the Incarnation was to constitute Christ a perfect mediator

between God and man, destined to offer a sacrifice of
redemption.

*"That same sacrifice was to be offered repeatedly in the
Church in the Sacrifice of the Mass. For this continuation
of His own sacrifice, Christ appointed men to share in His
own Priesthood...*

*"The Sacrament of orders is a social Sacrament which
has for its purpose not merely the sanctification of the
recipient but also the sanctification of the rest of the
Church through the powers this Sacrament confers. Since
it is wholly Divine in origin and impresses an indelible
character on its recipient, the Sacrament of Orders
definitively places the bishops and priests in a position of
higher rank than the laity."*[9]

In order that there be no question in anyone's mind
regarding the priesthood or that there can be any other
interpretation of this Truth, it is spelled out very clearly in
Canons on Holy Orders given to us by the Council of Trent,
which we will list, and also by Vatican Council II:

First, we quote from The Council of Trent:

1. "If anyone says that there is not a visible and
external priesthood in the New Testament, or that there
is no power of consecrating and offering the Body and
Blood of the Lord, and of remitting and of retaining
sins, but says that there is only the office and simple
ministry of preaching the gospel, or says that those who
do not preach are not priests at all: let him be anathema
(cursed).

2. "If anyone denies that in the Catholic Church,
besides the priesthood, there are other orders, both
major and minor, through which one must pass, as

---

[9]*Introduction to the Sacrament of Holy Orders* from *"The Church
Teaches"* by the Jesuit Fathers of St. Mary's College, St. Marys, Kansas.

through certain steps, towards the priesthood: let him be anathema.

3. "If anyone says that orders or holy ordination is not truly and properly a Sacrament instituted by Christ our Lord, or that it is a kind of human invention thought up by men inexperienced in ecclesiastical matters, or that it is only a kind of rite of choosing ministers of the word of God and the Sacraments: let him be anathema.

4. "If anyone says that by holy ordination the Holy Spirit is not given and thus it is useless for bishops to say 'Receive the Holy Spirit;' or if anyone says that no character is imprinted by ordination; or that he who was once a priest can become a layman again: let him be anathema.

5. "If anyone says that the sacred anointing which the Church uses at holy ordination not only is not required, but is despicable and harmful, just like other ceremonies: let him be anathema.

6. "If anyone says that in the Catholic Church there is no divinely instituted hierarchy consisting of bishops, priests and ministers: let him be anathema.

7. "If anyone says that bishops are not superior to priests, or that they do not have power to confirm and ordain, or says that the power they do have is common both to them and to priests; or says that the orders conferred by them are void without the consent and call of the people or of the secular power; or says that those who have not been rightly ordained by ecclesiastical and canonical power and have not been sent, but come from some other source, are lawful minsters of the Word and of the Sacraments: let him be anathema.

8. "If anyone says that bishops chosen by the authority of the Roman Pontiff are not legitimate and true bishops but a human invention: let him be anathema.

Then we quote from Vatican Council II:

"Christ, whom the Father has sanctified and sent into the world, has through His apostles, made their successors, the bishops, partakers of His consecration and His Mission.

"They have *legitimately* handed on to different individuals in the Church various degrees of participation in this Ministry. Thus the divinely established ecclesiastical ministry is exercised on different levels by those who from antiquity have been called bishops, priests and deacons.

"Priests, although they do not possess the highest degree of the priesthood (bishop), and although they are dependent on the bishops in the exercise of their power, nevertheless they are united with the bishops in sacerdotal dignity.

"By the power of the Sacrament of (Holy) Orders, in the image of Christ the eternal High Priest, they are consecrated to preach the Gospel and shepherd the faithful and to celebrate divine worship, so that they are true priests of the New Testament."[10]

There are those who say that Jesus never ordained the Apostles, that the Sacrament as we teach it, did not exist, and if it did, it was only for the Apostles and not their successors. This question was often put to us in an effort to confuse us because traditionally, Catholics have never been able to quote the Bible chapter and verse. But the actual act of Ordination is first found in Scripture in St. Paul's letters to Timothy, in which he reminds Timothy of his priestly obligations. In the first reference, we read:

"Do not neglect the gift you have, which was given you by prophetic utterance when the elders laid their hands upon you."[11]

---

[10]Lumen Gentium #28
[11]1Tim 4:14

Then in another passage, we read;

"Hence I remind you to rekindle the gift of God that is within you through the laying on of my hands; for God did not give us a spirit of timidity but a spirit of power and love and self-control."[12]

St. Gregory of Nyssa, an early Father of the Church, gave us an extremely inspiring image and unique teaching, in that he compared the priesthood to the Eucharist. He wrote:

"The self-same power of the Word makes the priest holy and venerable, for he is set apart from the rest of the community by the new blessing which he has received....

"As far as externals go, he is who he was; but his invisible soul is changed for the better by a certain invisible power and grace."[13]

With all these powers and all the graces coming to us through the ministry of Christ's priesthood, you have to know that this Sacrament, and these servants of Christ, would be the first to come under scorn by the enemy.

One of the greatest attacks on the Church which of itself became one of the greatest attacks on the priesthood came from Martin Luther, himself a priest, or at least he was prior to his excommunication by Pope Leo X in 1521. As part of Luther's attempt to destroy the Church, he maintained that all Christians are priests by their very Baptism, and through this Baptism all Christians could preach and administer the Sacraments. He was the major factor in challenging the sacrificial aspect of the mandate given the Apostles at the Last Supper. Also, one of the first things he did was to take priests and the priesthood out of his *new church*. He tried to do in one fell swoop what Satan

---

[12] 2Tim 1:6-7
[13] New Catholic Encyclopedia Vol 11-page 769

had been trying to do for centuries. He eliminated the priesthood.

Pope Paul III counteracted Luther's assault through the Council of Trent, by not only defining the priesthood, but condemning those who deny the power of the priesthood. The Council Fathers wrote,

> "*If anyone says there is no priesthood in the New Testament, or that there is no power of consecrating and of offering the true Body and Blood of the Lord, and of forgiving and retaining sins, but only the office and sheer ministry of preaching the Gospel,* **let him be anathema!**"[14]

In addition, the Council defined that the rite of Ordination is "*a true and proper Sacrament instituted by Christ*" and not merely "*a rite of sorts for choosing ministers of the word of God and of the Sacraments.*"

The Old Testament also gives credence to the exclusivity of the ordained priesthood. In the opening of section II of Article 6 of the Catechism of the Catholic Church, The Sacrament of Holy Orders, the authors quote from the Old Testament in regard to a *special* priesthood:

> "The chosen people was constituted by God as 'a kingdom of priests and a holy nation.' But within the people of Israel, God chose one of the twelve tribes, that of Levi, and set it apart for liturgical service; God Himself is its inheritance. A special rite consecrated the beginnings of the priesthood of the Old Covenant. The priests are 'appointed to act on behalf of men in relation to God, to offer gifts and sacrifices for sins.'"[15]

Also we read in the same section of the Catechism of the Catholic Church, "The liturgy of the Church...sees in the priesthood of Aaron and the service of the Levites, as in the

---

[14]condemned, cursed
[15]Catechism of the Catholic Church #1539

institution of the seventy elders,[16] a prefiguring of the ordained ministry of the *New Covenant*."

The battle rages!   Although the Royal priesthood according to the order of Melchizedek has always been under siege and the Church has always fought against those heresies, the invectives spewed at the Body of Christ through this disobedient Judas[17] was the first to cause a real break in the solidity and unity of the Church.

The attacks on the priesthood continue because they *have* to continue, in whatever way Satan thinks will be most successful in destroying these specially chosen Soldiers of Christ.   But we have to know that Satan is after us, the people of God. The priest is just the means the Lord uses to walk us through our pilgrimage of life into the Kingdom of God. Satan has been trying to destroy the priesthood from the very First Century in an effort to leave us hopeless and helpless. The battle is between God and the devil, between the Angels of God and the fallen angels.

Therefore take up the armor of God, that you may be able to resist in the evil day, and stand in all things perfect."[18]

In the History of our Church, the roles of those brave martyrs who were butchered because of their Priesthood and in defense of their beliefs, is long and sad. It is a badge of courage our priests will wear in glory as they enter the Kingdom as an unbeatable force, Soldiers of Christ.

There have been so many Martyrs down through the centuries, many of them priests who would not give up their Church. Pick an age, any age in the history of the world, and this stands true. Nazi Germany and Stalinist Russia, China under Mao-Tse-Tung in this century, Mexico under the Masonic government of Plutarco Elías Calles in the 1920's,

---

[16]Num 11:24-25
[17]Luther
[18]Eph 6:13

France during the French Revolution and under Napoleon Bonaparte, England and Ireland under Henry VIII and his successors, Japan in the Eighteenth Century, the Middle East under the Saracens, China under the Communists, Poland under Nazism and Communism; the list is endless. Any time the Lord begins to touch people through the hands of His priests, His representatives "*In Persona Christi*" on earth, Satan attacks furiously. The carnage is outrageous.

Satan has been trying to destroy the Church since Jesus walked the earth. Our Lord promised us that the gates of Hell would not prevail against the church.[19] But that has not stopped the evil one from trying to make it happen. His greatest triumph would be to make a liar out of God.

This may explain in part why there has been such a furious assault on the Priesthood especially in this century. If we follow the history of the Church down through the ages, we find that Satan's way of trying to destroy the Priesthood was very simple and systematic; kill all the priests.

But that's not the enemy's only blueprint to destroy the people of God by annihilating the priests of God. One which has proven very effective is by discrediting the priest by mounting smear campaigns which destroy character and reputations. Many of our priests cannot stand up against the glare of public outrage. Granted, some of the charges against our priests are true. But for every true charge of impropriety are ten which are fabricated. For every proven case of sexual misconduct of a lay person which winds up on the back page of a local newspaper, and never makes it on the six o'clock news, an accusation against a priest will always make headlines on the front page, and lead-in copy on TV news.

That's bad. Both accounts we've given you above, that of the tyrants of the world massacring our priests and

---

[19]Mt 16:18

religious *physically,* and the tyrants of the media slaughtering their *names* and *reputations* have succeeded in bringing the ranks of religious in our Church to an all-time low. And while they're at it, not only the members of our Church, but every denomination of Christianity is being attacked violently and brutally decimated in one way or another. So the enemy has come up with a good plan to thin out our ranks. And we have to get down on our knees and pray for those priests, brothers and nuns who are feeling the pressure of the world. We have to be their strength.

However, that's not the worst of it. They can kill us, but they can't make us betray Our Lord Jesus. But there are those who would destroy us from within, the great Apostasy.

The priesthood is being minimized by some priests; we're being told there is nothing special about the priest. We're being victimized by the enemy from within, the Satan of peer pressure. The priest is being told he's not from the Order of Melchizedek; he's not up there on any pedestal or at least shouldn't be. He's not something special; he's just one of us, and many of the feminists would have us believe that our priests today don't have the zeal, the fervor, the love of their vocation; they're just going through the motions, and so they should be replaced by women who care more about offering the Sacrifice of the Mass than these tired old men; therefore these women should be the priests.

The flame of the Holy Spirit has to be put back into our priesthood. Our priests must be affirmed. We must tell them how important they are to us. We as a Church cannot survive without them. Do you tell your priest how you appreciate his priesthood, the ongoing sacrifice he makes for us? When was the last time you thanked your priest for celebrating the Mass? Do you pay attention when he preaches from the pulpit? Have you ever told him how much his homily meant to you? Do you love your priests? Do you love Jesus? *Save the priesthood!*

Every time, we read this ordination prayer card, given to us by a young priest who has since left the Priesthood, we could cry and cry and cry! We need you, our dear *Ambassadors of Christ*; we love you; Jesus loves you! Jesus wants you! Jesus needs you!

> *To live*
>> *in the midst of the world*
>> *without wishing its pleasures;*
> *To be a member of each family,*
>> *yet belong to none.*
> *To share all sufferings,*
> *To heal all wounds,*
> *To penetrate all secrets.*
> *To go from men to God and*
>> *offer Him their prayers;*
> *To return from God to men*
>> *to bring pardon and hope.*
> *To have a heart of fire for charity*
>> *and a heart of bronze for chastity;*
> *To teach and to pardon,*
> *To console and to bless always-*
> *My God, what a life! and it is Yours,*
>> *O priest of Jesus Christ.*

-Lacordaire

Above:
Council of Constantinople
The Councils have always been a guiding force in our Church

Above:
Second Vatican Council
The Second Vatican Council was our most recent council.
Many of the documents that came from this council are still being
studied and implemented today.

The Holy Spirit in the Councils

The Church condemns a Heresy and defines a Truth!

It looks as if hell is about to prevail against Mother Church, the Holy Spirit inspires the Pope to call an Ecumenical Council! *You have a treasure!* I can still hear the Lord speaking to our hearts when it looked as if we were about to lose everything.[1]

Yes we have not one treasure, but many! And one of the greatest Treasures, the Lord has given us is also a most powerful weapon against Heresy and for Truth, that of the Ecumenical (Universal) Councils.

"An Ecumenical Council is an official assembly of all the bishops of the world, which, when summoned by the Bishop of Rome, the Pope, constitutes the *highest teaching authority* in the Church. These Councils have always been called at crucial times in the history of the Church."[2]

The justification for calling these Councils of the Church, down through the ages, comes from Jesus' mandate to Peter and the Apostles, in which they were given the power to teach and to discipline.[3] The members of the Council are given a supernatural power by Christ, and through the merits of Christ given Him by the Father. Our Lord Jesus is there, guiding and protecting the Pope and his bishops. It is a *Dogma of the Church* that when a Council issues a document approved by the Pope, the Holy Spirit envelops the Council and prevents it from making any formal error. The Lord may allow us to go through our paces, but He will always be there, until the end of time.[4]

"'The Roman Pontiff, head of the college of bishops, enjoys this infallibility in virtue of his office, when, as

---

[1]when the Lord inspired Bob & Penny to write: *This is My Body, This is My Blood, Miracles of the Eucharist.*
[2]Catholic History and Dictionary OSV 1995
[3]Mt 16:17-19
[4]Mt 28:20

supreme pastor and teacher of the faithful - who confirms his brethren in the faith - he proclaims a definitive act a doctrine pertaining to faith or morals....The infallibility promised to the Church is also present in the body of the bishops when, together with Peter's successor, they exercise the supreme Magisterium,' above all in an Ecumenical Council.[5] When the Church through its supreme Magisterium proposes a doctrine 'for belief as being divinely revealed,' and as the teaching of Christ, the definitions 'must be adhered to with the obedience of faith.' This infallibility extends as far as the deposit of Divine Revelation itself."[6]

Councils have usually been convened for two basic reasons: (1) to teach about the Church and (2) to condemn heresies against the Church. But although a particular heresy may have been condemned by a given Council, it sometimes took many centuries and many Councils before that particular heresy was effectively stamped out.

Arianism is a perfect example:

The **Council of Nicaea in 325**, the first major Ecumenical Council, condemned *Arianism*,[7] that great heresy which among other things, denied the Divinity of Jesus. *This heresy taught that Jesus was not God the Son, that He was created out of nothing; He did not exist with the Father together with the Holy Spirit before the beginning of time. By its nature, it also had to deny the Trinity.*

In condemning this heresy, the Truth the Council defined was the Nicene Creed, which we profess each

---

[5]Vatican Council I

[6]Catechism of the Catholic Church, #891

[7]More on this and other heresies down through the ages, can be found in Bob & Penny's book: *Scandal of the Cross and Its Triumph, Heresies throughout the History of the Church.*

Sunday at Mass to this day. It is a synopsis of what we believe. But it didn't really stop the heresy.

The **4th Council of Chalcedon in 451** not only affirmed the Council of Nicaea in its condemnation of Arianism, which had not yet died despite the condemnation 125 years before, it defined the two natures, Divine and human, in the One Divine Person of Christ. This was extremely successful in that it weakened their position, lost them much credibility, and consequently created a furor among the Arians.

The **5th Council of Constantinople in 553** was called to reaffirm the Council of Chalcedon and condemn Arianism in defending the Council of Chalcedon, which it did.

The **6th Council of Constantinople in 681** reaffirmed both the previous Councils by proclaiming the doctrine of the two wills and the two natural energies in Christ, the Divine and the human, as two distinct entities, undivided, inseparable, and without confusion.

It took four Councils, over a period of 356 years, to finally put down a major heresy, *Arianism*, in its original form. However, there are cults and sects who still follow the Arian heresy. But you can see from this how each succeeding Council affirmed a previous Council. It is a fact that since Councils are protected by the Holy Spirit, no error can come from one of them, and therefore, no Council will ever negate a previous Council.

Unquestionably one of the most important Councils the Church ever convened was the **Council of Trent in 1545**. Embers from the fires of Hell found their way to the surface of the earth through self-seeking nobility in Germany who used the dissidence and disobedience of a disenchanted Augustinian monk - Martin Luther - to attack the Church and steal Papal properties. Money, power, and hate of the Catholic Church ignited the fires which scorched the earth and burned everyone and everything in their path. We will not go into the Protestant Reformation in this chapter, as we have devoted a great deal to it in Book II of the Trilogy, *Tragedy of the Reformation*. Let it suffice to say that there were more reasons for it than appeared on the surface.

There were two main reasons for the Council of Trent:

First, Pope Leo X in 1521, condemned forty-one of Martin Luther's propositions, and then in January of the following year excommunicated him. But because they were not done under the auspices of an Ecumenical Council, they were not accepted universally by everyone in the Church.

Second, the Council was called and did clearly define teachings of the Church which had been under attack by Martin Luther and his followers. This Council, most notably, gave us affirmation of all the Sacraments, in particular Baptism, Original Sin, the Eucharist under both Species, and the Sacrament of Matrimony, as well as proclaiming the Mass a *Sacrifice* - the ongoing Sacrifice of the Cross, Holy Scripture as a rule of faith, Justification through faith and works, disciplinary reform of the bishops - correcting many abuses, and the Establishment of Seminaries.

The first thing this Council did was reaffirm the Nicene Creed. Next it laid. down sources of revealed Truths *on Sacred Scripture* and the unwritten *tradition* handed down by the Apostles, which provided the foundation for all its subsequent rulings. This was the basis for the Council. You must remember what they were fighting: Luther's *Sola Scriptura*, or *"If it's in the Bible, I believe it. If it's not, I don't,"* theology. Never mind the fact that some of the Scripture passages had been rewritten by Luther to accommodate his own agenda. So now Pope Paul III,[8] twenty-four years after Pope Leo X condemned Luther's forty-one propositions, covered his bases well, supplying a clear foundation of what our Church believes in and teaches; this has been of

---

[8]the Pope who convened the Council of Trent

invaluable help throughout the centuries following, defining and defending the Truths of our Church.

The supplementation of this Council produced works similar to what was released after Vatican Council II.

A revised Index of Forbidden Books was published in 1564.

A Roman Catechism for Pastors was published in 1566.

The Reformed Roman Breviary was published in 1568.

The Reformed Roman Missal was published in 1570.

This Council seemed to be the Catholic answer to the Protestant Reformation. It's important to remember, the rank and file members of the Church didn't know what was happening, other than there was a rumble in the Church. Doctrines were being denied and questioned in an unbridled, reckless way. The Council was the Church's way of clearly differentiating Catholic Doctrine from Protestantism.

It was important at that time, and is till today, to tell the people of God that there is an element contradicting Catholic doctrine which has been trying to proselytize Catholics and take them away from the True Church. The Protestants were successful in that the Catholic Church lost 6,000,000 believers in Europe. But the Church fought back and will fight for her lambs, Our Lord raising up holy Popes to lead us and guide us to victory. The Council of Trent turned out to be a blessing in that our doctrines were clearly defined, so that we would understand beyond a doubt what we believe.

Teachings from that time to this, come from the basis laid down in these Councils, and in particular, the Council of Trent. If you read the Catechism of the Catholic Church, today, you will see the many references regarding the Sacraments, the Church's teachings on Heaven, Hell and Purgatory, as well as a Treasury of Truths and doctrines, and they all come from the various Councils. All this forms a part of our Catholic Faith and makes up our Deposit of Faith, the Magisterium of the Church.

The basic Truths defined by the various Councils have been an area of conflict with our separated brothers and sisters, for the last 500 years. But we did not separate from them and Truths that had come down from the centuries; it was they who left us and renounced the Church which dates back to Jesus and the first Apostles. We love our brethren, but to accommodate them we would have to reject the Faith passed down by our Church from our sweet Christs on earth - our Popes - in unbroken succession for the last 2000 years, and confine our beliefs to *individual* interpretations of the Bible,[9] denying the power of the Holy Spirit working through the Church down through the ages. If we limit everything we believe to that which ended with John's book of Revelation, written about the year 80 A.D., we deny the power of the Holy Spirit working through the Councils.

Like an Honor Roll Call, let us call off the twenty-one Ecumenical Councils, the Church has recognized in the 2,000 years since Jesus ascended into Heaven. They are:

1. **Nicaea I,** 325 A.D.- Condemned Arianism.[10]

2. **Constantinople I**, 381 A.D.- Condemned the Macedonians and declared the Holy Spirit consubstantial with the Father and the Son.

3. **Ephesus,** 431 A.D. - Condemned the heretical sects of Nestorianism and Pelagianism.

Pelagius wrote: "*God has given men freedom of will so that by purity and sinlessness of life* (a life without sinning), *they may become like God.*" and "*A man chaste and sinless has received from God the power to become a son of God.*"[11,12]

---

[9]thus the reason for 40,000 denominations, all of whom claim they believe solely in the Bible.

[10]for a detailed explanation of this and all the heresies, read Bob and Penny Lord's book, *Scandal of the Cross and Its Triumph*

[11]The Faith of the Early Fathers - W.A. Jurgens

Pelagius exaggerated the natural powers of man, claiming man was the master of his own destiny. He taught that *God cannot do anything that man cannot do.*[13] He denied the existence of a supernatural condition; he denied the existence of God! [Do we not hear this today, under a new name, *New Age?*]

The Nestorian sect was founded by *Nestorius*, a priest and monk chosen by Emperor Theodosius as Archbishop of Constantinople. He taught a version of Arianism. He maintained that Christ the *human* died on the Cross, not the Second Person of the Trinity and the Son of God. By denying the Divinity of Christ, he had to deny the title of our Lady as Mother of God (Theotokos in Greek) by the same action. Although the Council of Ephesus condemned this heresy, it wasn't until *1100 years later* that the Nestorians were united with the Roman Church.

[Author's note: You can see from all these heresies how the damage done lives on far beyond the heretic. In some instances, the heretic repented of his heresy, but it lived on for hundreds of years after the fact. We must be so careful to what we subject our brothers and sisters. This is one of the reasons we don't encourage individual interpretation of the Bible. Our Protestant brothers and sisters have done that for over 400 years, and we have somewhere in the area of 40,000 religious sects and cults, all of whom state that they believe in what is in the Bible. If that is so, why are there so many thousands of sects who disagree with each other's interpretation of the Bible?]

4. **Chalcedon,** 451 A.D. - Condemned Monophysitism - which denied the dual nature of Jesus, God and man. This was condemned by defining the two natures of Christ, a

---

[12] part of today's New Age philosophy
[13] Mormonism teaches this

Divine Nature consubstantial[14] with God and a human nature consubstantial with us.

[Author's Note: You can also see from all these Councils how the Church we have today was formed on its feet; in other words, a doctrine was not necessarily defined authoritatively until it was attacked. We had no need to define the two natures of Jesus, or the three natures of the Trinity, until someone challenged them. So the Church evolved as these Councils defined Dogma. If we didn't have these Councils, protected by the Holy Spirit, we would not have the rich treasures of the Church we have today.]

5.   **Constantinople II**, 553 A.D. - condemned the Three Chapters, ruling that parts of the writings of three churchmen of Antioch, Theodore of Mopuestia, Theodoret of Cyr and Ibas of Edessa were filled with Nestorian philosophy, which had formerly been condemned. In actuality, this was a re-affirmation of the condemnation of the heresy *Nestorianism*. During the Council it was determined that the writing attributed to Ibas of Edessa was in fact written by someone else.

6.   **Constantinople III**, 680 A.D. - Condemned the heresy of *Monothelitism* which denied the two natures of Jesus, Divine and human. It also censured Pope Honorius I. He was criticized by the Council for writing two letters ordering silence on the subject, while refusing to come out with a definitive statement about the question raised by the Monothelitists. [Author's note: This was just prior to the Greek Schism and this Council took place in the East. There was a great deal of antagonism on both sides, the East against the West and vice-a-versa. While the Pope was

---

[14]a term given to us by the Council of Nicaea which is used to differentiate the three Persons of the Trinity. The Council of Chalcedon used the same term to differentiate between the two natures of Jesus, Divine and human.

remiss in not making a statement at that time, it was a slight to him and his office for anyone to criticize or censure him.]

7.   **Nicaea II**, 787 A.D. - condemned Iconoclasm (Image-breaking) a heresy which was begun by an emperor, stating that the veneration of images was blasphemous, maintaining that it stopped the Jews and Muslims from converting to Catholicism because they could never venerate images. The Church came against it through St. John of Damascene and Pope Gregory VIII, who condemned Iconoclasm. This did not stop the emperor and his sons from continuing to destroy images, the veneration of which they claimed to be superstitious. The popes on the other hand continued to condemn the image-breaking until the Second Council of Nicaea finally condemned the heresy officially.

8.   **Constantinople IV**, 869 A.D. - Condemned Photius, a fiery patriarch of Constantinople who deposed the Pope (at least as far as the Eastern Church was concerned) and declared him "anathema,"[15] by which he excommunicated the Pope for apostasy. Obviously this did not hold ground[16] because Photius was condemned and deposed as Patriarch. At this point, the Emperor and the Pope truly believed that the problems with the Greek church were finished. But that was not so, as the problem with East and West would resurface in 1054, leading to the Greek Schism.

9.   **Lateran I**, 1123 - Issued decrees on:

Simony: selling of spiritual things, such as healings, miracles and etc. It stems from Simon Magus who tried to buy spiritual powers from Sts. Peter and Paul.

Celibacy: Forbids marriage among clergy, and normally excludes married men from ordination.

Lay investiture: A right taken by secular leaders, kings, rulers, etc., whereby they would invest abbots and bishops

---

[15]cursed

[16]As he lacked the authority to do so; no one may depose a Pope.

from among friends and nobility for favors, usually property and money.

It also confirmed the Concordat of Worms in that it resolved the Lay Investiture problem by which only clergy could elect bishops and abbots. They could not be appointed by nobility or royalty.

10. **Lateran II**, 1139 - ended a papal Schism which had been brought about by the election of two Popes at the same time, Innocent II and Anacletus II. The schism ended with the death of the latter pope (an antipope). Excommunicating followers of Pope Anacletus II for their heretical teachings, the council also condemned and reformed abuses which had taken place with regard to the Eucharist, Infant Baptism, the priesthood and marriage; prohibition of payment for Confirmation, Extreme Unction and burials, nuns failing to live by their rules, and many other abuses.

11. **Lateran III**, 1179 - Ended another Papal Schism similar to the one of Lateran II in 1139. It also condemned the heresies of *Albigensianism*. Albigensianists believed in two Gods; one good and the other evil. They rejected all the Sacraments, in particular Matrimony and the Real Presence of Jesus in the Eucharist. Sexual permissiveness was encouraged, but pregnancy was to be avoided at all costs. They took the worst of old heresies from centuries gone by and incorporated them into one.

The Council also condemned *Waldensianism*. This group rejected all the Sacraments but Baptism and the Eucharist. They rejected indulgences, penances and fasting. They felt the Church was in need of major reform, and maintained a contempt for the authority of the church. They believed the priests had no authority. They scoffed at Purgatory and refused to observe the teachings of the Church.

12. **Lateran IV**, 1215 - Considered the most important Council prior to the Council of Trent. It repeated the Condemnation of *Albigensianism and Waldensianism*. Privileges previously given to crusaders were added to those fighting against heretics - planned a Crusade which lost its impetus after the death of the Pope Innocent III in 1216. The obligation of all Catholics to go to Confession and receive Communion at least once a year was mandated at this Council, as well as a definition of Transubstantiation.[17] The Council also dealt with abuses in the Church which were prevalent at that time.

13. **Lyons I**, 1245 - The major reason for convening this Council was to condemn and excommunicate Emperor Frederick II, who had persecuted the Church and its leaders, and continually confiscated Papal lands. An indicator of how terrified everyone was of him, very few German or Sicilian bishops came to the Council, for fear of being arrested on their way. Frederick was also deposed as Holy Roman Emperor.

14. **Lyon II**, 1274 - The Church was reunited with the Greek Church through this Council which felt the need for unification with the Eastern Church because of the Crusades, which were still going on. But the union did not last. Other abuses were addressed and disciplinary reforms put into effect.

15. **Vienne**, 1311 - Abolished the Knights Templar. This was one of the first and most powerful Religious Orders of the Middle Ages, who had taken vows of Military protection of the Church and its properties, mostly in the Holy Land. A greedy King Philip of France, who coveted the Knights' money and lands, created a scandal about them, and forced the Pope, who was weak, to abolish the order and turn over

---

[17]Conversion of bread and wine into the Body and Blood of Our Lord Jesus during the Consecration of the Mass. Only the *appearance* of bread and wine remain, but the substance has been changed.

their lands and money to the King. The abolition of the Knights took place at this Council. This Council also enacted reforms.

16. **Constance,** 1414 - Ended the Great Western Schism in which a split in the Church came about because two Popes reigned - a Pope and an antipope. Countries pledged their allegiance to one or the other of the two Popes, based on the political advantage. It was a disastrous situation which was only rectified at this Council by which the Avignon antipope finally relinquished power to the Roman Pope.

This Council also condemned John Hus, a Czech reformer very influenced by British heretic, John Wycliff. Hus denied the Primacy of Peter and preached Predestination. He went before the Council of Constance, where he was condemned to death and burned at the stake.

17. **Basel, Ferrara, Florence,** 1431 - Originally convened in Basel, Switzerland with the purpose of effecting reforms within the Church, it became bogged down because of a heated debate over papal supremacy. It was dissolved and moved to Ferrara, Italy, where the controversy flared up again between bishops. It was finally resolved by a session in Florence, Italy. It reformed legislation, coming out against concubinage[18] of the clergy, moved to call more local synods, and established of a new set of norms to be used in choosing a new Pope, and formulating election procedures. One of the main concerns was to resolve the controversy with the followers of Hus and the Greek Church.

18. **Lateran V**, 1512 - This was called by Pope Julius II in opposition to an attempted Council called in Pisa by dissident bishops in league with King Louis XII of France who was having a major altercation with the Pope. The Council of Pisa was not well-attended and was considered a

---

[18]The enduring state or practice of sexual intercourse between a man and a woman not bound to each other by legitimate marriage.

failure. However, one of the attempted documents of that Council was to suspend Pope Julius II. Naturally, the Pope condemned the actions of the Council of Pisa, and so he called the Fifth Lateran Council in 1512.

The Council also condemned a document called the *Pragmatic Sanction of Bourges*, which was issued in Bourges, France, by the French clergy under the control of the then King Charles VII against the Pope. In it, the French Clergy or the monarchy formalized the *rights* of the clergy *against* the *Papacy*; gave the Church of France (or king of France) control over Ecclesiastical appointments (ordaining Bishops) and the right to *determine the validity of a Papal Bull*. This was totally unacceptable behavior on the part of the French Church and the French king, and while it was revoked by the next king of France, Louis XI in 1461, it was merely tokenism. The practice dragged on by succeeding kings and clergy in France until this Council formally condemned it in 1516 by the Concordat of Bologna, signed by the French King Francis I and Pope Leo X, who took over from Julius II.

This Council also condemned the heresies of one Pietro Pomponazzi, who taught according to the philosophy of Aristotle various heresies among which were that miracles were impossible and the soul was mortal, perishing after death.

19. **Trent**, 1545 - This Council has been called the most important Ecumenical Council called in the history of the Church. We wrote about this at the beginning of the chapter.

20. **Vatican Council I** - Held from December 8, 1869 to September 1, 1870, it was probably the shortest Ecumenical Council. It took place during the height of the Italian War for Independence, or Risorgimento, which ultimately took all the Papal States away from the Vatican.

This has possibly been the most understated and misunderstood of all the Ecumenical Councils. It was spearheaded by Pope Pius IX, who was exalted much like our dear Pope John Paul II. Those who loved him revered him as a Saint during his lifetime; those who hated him *"criticized him as a vain autocrat and unintelligent puppet."* Pope Pius IX was the Lord's powerful servant who held onto the values and traditions of our Faith against unbelievable attacks from the enemy. Originally passionately sympathetic to the cause of Italians suffering the tyranny of Austria, under whose heel Italy had been suppressed, he separated himself from all things political and concentrated his Papacy on being pastor and spiritual leader of his flock.

His rule took place at a time when the Papal States were being taken away from the Papacy by the very brothers he had defended, the Italian zealots who had fought for independence and unity. After the Papal States had been taken away from him, and Rome was invaded and occupied by the Italian forces, Pope Pius IX considered himself less a dethroned sovereign than a custodian of the property which had been given to the Papacy by Catholics down through the centuries, and for which he claimed responsibility. He never accepted what had been done to the Papal States, and to the end of his Pontificate, considered himself a prisoner in the Vatican, all that was left of the Vatican States.

Two extremely important achievements came from Pope Pius IX through Vatican I. One was the Dogma of the Infallibility of the Pope, called *Pastor Aeternus.* This was extremely important at a crucial time in the history of the Church when all authority of the Pontiff was being threatened by destruction from powers without and within.

The other doctrine, called *Dei Filius*, Son of God, was possibly *the* most important work of Pope Pius IX. It affirmed all the Truths of the Church. *[This from the man who gave us the Dogma of the Immaculate Conception in*

1854, which had been prefaced personally by Our Lady to St. Catherine Labouré at the Chapel of the Miraculous Medal in Paris in 1830 and was then confirmed subsequently by Our Lady personally to St. Bernadette at Lourdes, France in 1858.]

Pope Pius IX had come against major heresies which had found their way down to the rank and file from as early as the Renaissance, and then the Age of Reason and the Age of Enlightenment. He wrote an Encyclical against them on December 8, 1864, on the tenth Anniversary of his Dogma of the Immaculate Conception. It was entitled *Quanta cura*, which means "With Great Care." With this document, and the *Syllabus of Errors*, which became a part of it, Pope Pius IX systematically dealt with ten major categories of concern which were either wreaking havoc on the Church or separating us. They are as follows:

1. Pantheism, Naturalism and Absolute Rationalism
2. Moderate Rationalism
3. Indifferentism and Latitudinarianism
4. Socialism, Communism, Secret Societies, Bible Societies and Liberal-Clerical Societies
5. The Church and Its Rights
6. Civil Society and Its Relation to the Church
7. Natural and Christian Ethics
8. Christian Marriage
9. The Temporal Powers of the Pope
10. Modern Liberalism

Two days after he published this, he announced that there would be an Ecumenical Council to the cardinals in his Curia. He knew that the only way this encyclical and its Syllabus of Errors would have the strength necessary for it to be enforced in the Church would be through a Council.

It's almost as if he could predict what was about to happen to the strength of the Church in its relationship with the secular world. In an effort to protect the Church against the eventuality of losing its lands and much of its temporal power, he added some things to the Encyclical dealing with the relationship between the Church and the Secular Government, emphasizing the Divine Foundation of the Church and its full independence from all secular authority.[19]

The latter proved to be fruitless in the wake of an attack by Garibaldi's troops against Papal Rome. In 1861 Victor Emmanuele II had been crowned King and his main focus was to reunite all of Italy, part of which included the confiscation of all the Papal States from the Vatican. The French troops which had been protecting the Pope and the Vatican States, had to leave to fight in the Franco-Prussian War. Rome was overrun by Victor Emmanuele's troops. The situation was hopeless; the Pope adjourned the Council in haste. He never ended it; it was just not reconvened. The Pope never accepted the takeover of the Papal lands and died proclaiming he was a hostage of the Vatican.

But the Pope did great things during his Pontificate. His Dei Filius, reaffirming the teachings of the Church, was a brilliant move by the Pope to slow down the tide of *Modernism* which had already found its way into the Church on a major scale. We believe this dear Pope was given discernment about the tide of blasphemy which would be precipitated by the rise of Secularism, and the dreaded Modernism movement which his successor Pope St. Pius X would come against and condemn at the beginning of the Twentieth Century. Our dear saintly Pope Pius X thought he had destroyed Modernism with his encyclical, *Lamentabili sane exitu* in April 1907 and *Pascendi dominici gregis* in November of the same year. However, Modernism has never gone away; to the contrary, it has reared its evil head very strongly after Vatican Council II.

---

[19]Separation of Church and State, as you can see was begun by the Church to keep the State from interfering with the Church, not to keep Christ and His Church from interfering with the State.

21. **Vatican Council II**, 1962 - Pope John XXIII instituted the Council on January 25, 1959, the Feast of the Conversion of St. Paul by telling the Cardinals assembled his reasons for wanting to convene a Council. One of them was simply because with the exception of Vatican Council I, which only lasted a year and was not able to do everything which Pope Pius IX desired to accomplish, there had not been a Council convened for 400 years. There had been much change in the Church and the world in that time. As plans proceeded for the Council, he expressed a desire to "*Open the windows of the Church and let the Holy Spirit in.*" He talked about a new Pentecost, and updating the Church to modern times. He saw an opening of the way for reunion with the separated brothers of the East and West. [As Cardinal Roncali, Pope John XXIII was Apostolic Nuncio to Constantinople in Turkey for many years. He had a great rapport with the Greek Orthodox.]

The Council opened on October 11, 1962. Pope John XXIII died in June 1963, shortly after the Council began. The bulk of the credit for what resulted from Vatican II goes to Pope Paul VI who was responsible for overseeing the proceedings until their end in 1965.

There were many accomplishments attributed to Vatican II. One which had been planned since the Council of Trent was a true definition of the Church. It had been part of Pope Pius IX's agenda for Vatican Council I, but because of the political situation of the time was never able to be accomplished. Vatican Council II gave us *Lumen Gentium*, the Dogmatic Constitution of the Church. Its declared purpose was to explain the Church's nature as a "*sign and instrument...of communion with God and of unity among all men*" and to define the Church's universal mission as the Sacrament of Human Salvation: "*This is the sole Church of Christ which in the Creed we profess to be one, holy, catholic and apostolic...*"

Many of the changes we see in the Church today came from Vatican Council II, such as Mass in the Vernacular rather than in Latin, a Novus Ordo, or New Order of the Mass, the Altar facing the people rather than facing the Tabernacle, more participation by the Congregation in the Mass, focus on the Celebration rather than Sacrificial aspect of the Mass, Sex Education, the right of dissent[20] and many others.

Those of us who have been alive since Vatican II, have seen confusion and concern, trying to discern between what some *say* is meant by the documents of Vatican II, according to what they call the *Spirit of Vatican II*, and what the documents *really say*, with some teaching what *they* believe Vatican II said, even if what they believe doesn't come from the Documents.

†

We could spend all our lives just learning about our inheritance from God the Father and Our Lord Jesus through the power of the Holy Spirit. It all came to us from the Trinity in one way or another, either directly from the words of Jesus, or through the inspiration of the Holy Spirit in the various Councils which have been convened down through the centuries.

Thanks to our Ecumenical Councils, we have condemned *heresy* and defined *Truth*. Now we just have to live that Truth and maintain that Truth. Praise Jesus in all things.

---

[20]The right of dissent was abolished during the pontificate of Pope John Paul II

Faith without good works...

"Take the case, my brothers, of someone who has never done a single good act but claims that he has faith. Will that faith save him? If one of the brothers or one of the sisters is in need of clothes and has not enough food to live on, and one of you says to them, 'I wish you well; keep yourself warm and eat plenty,' without giving them these bare necessities of life, then what good is that? Faith is like that: *if good works do not go with it, it is quite dead.*"

"...You say you have faith and I have good deeds; I will prove to you that I have faith by showing you my good deeds - now you prove to me that you have faith without any good deeds to show.

"...*Do realize, you senseless man, that faith without good works is useless!*"[1]

James the Apostle was very adamant about the need of good works, *centuries before Martin Luther changed Scripture to suit his own agenda.* St. Paul in his letter to the Romans wrote,

"*Now we know that what the law says is addressed to those under the law, so that every mouth may be silenced and whole world stand accountable to God since no human being will be justified in His sight by observing the law; for through the law comes consciousness of sin. But now the righteousness of God has been manifested apart from the law, though testified to by the law and the prophets. The righteousness of God through faith in Jesus Christ for all to believe. For there is no distinction; all have sinned and are deprived of the glory of God. They are justified freely by His grace through the redemption in Christ Jesus whom God set forth as an expiation, through faith, by His blood, to prove His righteousness because of the forgiveness of sins previously committed, through the*

---

[1]Jas. 2:14-18, 20

forbearance of God - to prove His righteousness in the present time, that He might be righteous and justify everyone who has faith in Jesus."[2]

According to the Catholic Encyclopedia,[3]

"Faith is the beginning of man's salvation, the foundation and root of all justification; without which it is impossible to please God and to obtain fellowship with His sons. Faith is man's assent to revealed truth. It is thus the basis of justification. We are justified by Christ and by good works, as declared in the Epistle of James."

Why did Paul make such a big thing about justification through faith in Jesus? The Pharisees, of which he had been a part, had put aside the covenant theology which the Israelites had always had with God from the time of Abraham and Moses (*"I will be their God and they will be My people"*). They set up a massive system of laws, by which man could achieve salvation. Relationship with God was not part of it; all they had to do was obey the laws. So the laws had become God in effect. Thus, justification was through following the law. God was completely out of the picture.

St. Paul even made reference to his status under the law. *"As regards the justice of the law, I was blameless."*[4] What he was saying was that as far as the Pharisee norm went, he was right on. But it had nothing to do with God. Once he became a Christian, he had to fight that philosophy, especially with regards to the Gentile converts. The Jewish converts, or Judaizers[5] fought Paul tooth and nail, and incited his gentile converts, telling them that they were not Christian unless they followed the Mosaic law.

---

[2]Rom 3:19-24

[3]Catholic Encyclopedia - Robert Broderick - Thomas Nelson Publishers

[4]Phil 3:6

[5]Heretics, supposed converts, Pharisees who had come to believe in Jesus, but really wanted the status quo of following Mosaic law.

There was a major dispute between St. Paul and the Judaizers in Antioch, regarding the Mosaic law. St. Peter was also involved in this. Paul saw the Jewish converts separating from the Gentile converts, including Sts. Peter and Barnabas. St. Paul could see everything he had worked for, all his teaching going right down the drain. He stood up in front of the assembly and challenged Peter and the others:

"We know that man is not justified by the works of the Law, but by the faith in Jesus Christ. Hence we also believe in Christ Jesus, that we may be justified by the faith of Christ, and not by the works of the law; because by the works of the Law no man will be justified."[6]

You can see from the above passage that when St. Paul made the statement that justification came through faith, it was meant to be faith apart from the burdensome laws that had been heaped upon the Israelites and the early Gentile converts.

St. James, on the other hand, may have been fighting the idea of his constituents that there was no need to do anything - that we were saved by the stripes of Jesus.

†††

Now here comes Luther who decided that the Church was too involved in works, selling indulgences and the like. He insisted that nothing man could do would help with his salvation, because man was intrinsically evil and could only be saved by guess what? *"the stripes of Jesus."* So he changed the Scripture passage of St. Paul to mean that salvation was by faith *alone* without good works. This was the basis for his teaching *"sola fide,"* Salvation through faith alone. He threw St. James out altogether. He wanted none of that good works stuff. That philosophy was also a good excuse to misbehave, do anything they wanted, because they would never be saved by anything they did or did not do, but by the

---

[6]Gal 2:16

Blood of Jesus. When you read the chapter on Luther in our *Trilogy, Book II - Tragedy of the Reformation*, you'll find that Luther *not only married a nun*, he insisted all religious give up their vows, especially of chastity.

The Council of Trent spent most of its council, and wrote most of its canons in opposition to the teachings of Luther, which had spread like wildfire, infecting all of Europe.

"If anyone says that all works performed before justification, regardless of how they were performed, are truly sins or merit God's hatred; or that the more zealously a person strives to dispose himself for grace, the more grievously he sins; let him be anathema."[7]

"If anyone says that a sinful man is justified by faith alone, meaning that no other cooperation is required to obtain the grace of justification, and that it is not at all necessary that he be prepared and disposed by the action of his will: let him be anathema."[8]

The Catechism of the Catholic Church teaches us:
"The works of mercy are charitable actions by which we come to the aid of our neighbor in his spiritual and bodily necessities. Instruction, advising, consoling, comforting are spiritual works of mercy, as are forgiving and bearing wrongs patiently. The corporal works of mercy consist especially in feeding the hungry, sheltering the homeless, clothing the naked, visiting the sick and imprisoned, and burying the dead. Among all these, giving alms to the poor is one of the chief witnesses to fraternal charity: it is also a work of justice pleasing to God."

St. Luke tells us: *"He who has two coats, let him share with him who has none; and he who has food must do likewise.*

---

[7]Canon 7 on Justification
[8]Canon 9 on Justification

But give for alms those things which are within; and behold, everything is clean for you.[9]

The Corporal works of Mercy, or as St. James said, *good works*, is alive and active in our Church. One of the greatest exponents of good works is the Legion of Mary. We find that many of the things in our Church which are recommended by Vatican II have been done by the Legion of Mary for years.

We'd like to share with you what we, as Legion of Mary did to perform Corporal Works of Mercy in our parish.

"Initially, all our friends from Marriage Encounter embraced the Legion of Mary. We met every Monday night in the rectory. We read from the Legion handbook, and prayed the Rosary. But there are those who are contemplative, and those who are action people. There are Marys, and there are Marthas. Penny and I are Marthas, although we have been trying for years to be more like Mary. After a few weeks of praying together, we asked our pastor what we, as the Legion of Mary, could do for him.

He said, "Go out into the community, door to door, and ask if any of the children of the Catholic Church are out there, who are not coming to church. And if you find them, tell them I long for them to return to Mother Church. Tell them we miss them; we're not a complete family until they and we are reunited."

We set out in pairs of two, as is required in the Legion. Being all Marriage Encounter couples, that was easy, and we were able to give the people a little something extra, the gift of our coupleness. We set out, hand in hand, probably rushing in where "angels fear to tread."

---

[9]Lk 3:11; 11:41

"We're here from St. Jude's. Are there any Catholics in your family?"

Either we looked kind of strange, or they did not expect to see Catholics coming door to door, or a little of both. We intrigued them. They not only did not slam the doors in our faces, but invited us in.

"Our pastor, Fr. Tom, asked us to call on all the homes and invite back any of our Catholic brothers and sisters who, for whatever reason, have left the Church." We a little nervously, ventured.

What began with what appeared to be curiosity on their parts, grew into interest, then into outright amazement.

"I used to be Catholic. When did this all begin, Catholics evangelizing, going door to door? I thought only Jehovah Witnesses and Mormons did that."

We smiled, and invited them to come to Mass, the Mass we attended, the next Sunday. Some came to the Masses. Others did not. Some returned to the Church for good. Others slipped back to where they had been. But for us, the Lord was working in our lives, and our Legion was working for our Parish. We were family. We were community. For those few weeks, the couples met and prayed together, went out and evangelized, bringing in the sheep for Father Tom. It was exciting."[10]

The Lord has much work for you to do. Don't worry about whether you are pleasing Him or if these works have to be done for your salvation. Jesus loves you; He will take care of you. ***Just do the work!***

---

[10]*We Came Back to Jesus* - Bob & Penny Lord 1988 - Page 118-119

Pray for the Souls in Purgatory

*"....before the Final Judgment, **there is a purifying fire.**
He who is Truth says that whoever utters blasphemy
against the Holy Spirit will be pardoned
neither in this age nor in the **age to come.**
From this sentence, we understand that certain offenses can be
forgiven in this age, but certain others in the age to come."*

St. Gregory the Great

†††

●Have you ever heard, *"Offer it up for the Souls in Purgatory?"*

●When was the last time you heard the expression *"Poor Souls in Purgatory?"*

●We were in Portland, Oregon last year giving a weekend of workshops on our new book, *Heaven, Hell and Purgatory.* When we began sharing on the Souls in Purgatory, we heard a voice from way in the back of the church. *"What's this about Purgatory? I haven't heard Purgatory mentioned for thirty years!"*

●Someone wrote us a letter, *"Don't tell me you're going back to the Church's old theology of fear with Purgatory?"*

●We were at an audience with His Holiness, Pope John Paul II this year. Bob was blessed to be able to kiss his hand and give him a copy of our book, *Visions of Heaven, Hell and Purgatory.* As Bob was kissing the Pope's hand, he could hear His Holiness reading the title, *"Fisions of Heafen, Hell und Poorgatory"* (Polish phonetic translation). His Holiness looked at Bob, smiled and shook his head in agreement.

So what do you think, family? Do you think it was about time we returned Purgatory to the front lines of the battleground? We think so, and by the affirmation we received from His Holiness; and the overwhelming response we have received on this book, making it a best seller, we believe we may have all thought the same thing.

Above:
The Chosen being given their crowns of glory as they leave Purgatory

Above: **Bob Lord presents Pope John Paul II a copy of**
"Visions of Heaven, Hell and Purgatory."

Purgatory is truly a Treasure of our Church. We thank our Lord Jesus for giving us that gift. Those who have made it, who have attained Heaven by way of Purgatory, have won the race. They were "*cleansed by the Blood of the Lamb.*"[1]

"Why put it in this book? We just wrote about a third of a book about Purgatory."[2] The consensus of opinion was *that exactly*, because Purgatory is truly a Treasure which our brothers and sisters in Christ do not accept, and it should be added to this book. Reading some of the comments from those within the Church,[3] our Protestant brothers and sisters are not the only ones who have to be taught about Purgatory. Our own dear parishes are not being taught about this most important Treasure.

†††

Purgatory and the Papal Authority of the Church

Let us begin by speaking about the authority of His Holiness Pope Paul III who, in company with his Bishops, declared on January 13, 1547, in the Council of Trent:[4]

"If anyone shall says that
after the reception of the grace of Justification,
to every penitent sinner the guilt is so remitted[5]
and the debt of eternal punishment so blotted out
that no penalty of temporal punishment remains to be discharged,
either in this world, or in the world to come in Purgatory,
before the entrance to the Kingdom of Heaven
can be opened to him:
let him be anathema (condemned)."

And if that was not enough, sixteen years and four Popes later, Pope Pius IV gathered his Bishops and Prelates

---

[1]Rev 7:14
[2]*Visions of Heaven, Hell and Purgatory*
[3]made at the beginning of this chapter
[4]Council of Trent DS 1680
[5]absolved, forgiven, pardoned

from the four corners of the world, commenced another Council of Trent[6] on December 4, 1563, and made this Decree on Purgatory at an Ecumenical Council:[7]

"Whereas the Catholic Church,
instructed by the Holy Spirit,
has, from the sacred writings,
and the ancient tradition of the Fathers,
taught in sacred Councils
and very recently in this Ecumenical Synod,
that there is a Purgatory
and the souls retained there are helped
by the suffrages[8] of the Faithful,
but particularly by the acceptable Sacrifice of the Altar[9]
the Holy Synod enjoins on Bishops
that they diligently endeavor
that the sound doctrine concerning Purgatory,
transmitted by the holy Fathers and sacred Councils,
be believed, maintained, taught,
and everywhere proclaimed by the Faithful of Christ."

So much for those within and without our Church who say there is no Purgatory. It sounds pretty simple to me: We are *required* to believe in Purgatory. And for those who might say that these are *old* pronouncements in *old* Councils, let us reiterate that no proclamation ever made by any Vatican Council has been nullified by a succeeding Council.

---

[6]Session XXV

[7]An Ecumenical Council is one to which all the bishops of the Catholic world and all other prelates or dignitaries entitled to vote, are invited to gather under the Presidency of the Pope or his representative. The decrees of an Ecumenical Council, when ratified by the Pope, are binding on all Christians. It is now sometimes called 'general council.' (The Catholic Encyclopedia - Broderick)

[8]additional prayers of the Divine Office for particular intentions. (The Catholic Encyclopedia - Broderick)

[9]The Sacrifice of the Mass which is the ongoing Sacrifice of the Cross

†††

Purgatory and Vatican Council II

"Until the Lord shall come in His majesty,
and all the Angels with Him and death being destroyed,
all things are subject to Him,
some of His disciples are exiles on earth,
*some having died are **purified**,*
and others are in glory beholding
'clearly God Himself Triune and One, as He is'
but all in various ways and degrees
are in communion in the same charity of God and neighbor
and all sing the same hymn of glory to our God.
For all who are in Christ, having His Spirit,
form one church and cleave together in Him.
Therefore the union of the wayfarers
with the brethren who have gone to sleep
in the peace of Christ
is not in the least weakened or interrupted,
but on the contrary,
according to the perpetual faith of the Church,
is strengthened by communication of spiritual goods."[10]

Fully conscious of this communion of the whole Mystical Body of Jesus Christ, the pilgrim Church from the very first ages of the Christian Religion, has cultivated with great piety, the memory of the dead, and *"because it is a holy and wholesome thought to pray for the dead that they may be loosed from their sins', also offers suffrages for them."*[11]

Purgatory and the Catechism of the Catholic Church

The Church of the Twentieth Century has this to say about Purgatory:[12]

---

[10]Lumen Gentium #49

[11]Lumen Gentium #50

[12]Section III of The Profession of Faith, Catechism of the Catholic Church - #1030-1031-1032

"All who die in God's grace and friendship,
but still imperfectly purified,
are indeed assured of their eternal salvation;
but after death they undergo purification,
so as to achieve the holiness necessary
to enter the joy of Heaven."

The Church gives the name *Purgatory* to this final purification of the elect, which is entirely different from the punishment of the damned. The Church formulated her doctrine of faith on Purgatory, especially at the *Councils of Florence and Trent.* The traditions of the Church, through Holy Scripture, speak of a cleansing fire.[13]

This section, while written in language for today, comes from those two Councils, and from one edict by Pope Benedict XII, who preceded both Councils:

"...the souls of all the saints...and other faithful who died
after receiving Christ's holy Baptism (provided they were
not in need of purification when they died,....or, if they then
did need or will need some purification, when they have
been purified after death),...have been, are and will be in
Heaven, in the Heavenly Kingdom and celestial paradise
with Christ, joined to the company of the Holy Angels..."[14]

Even the renowned pagan philosophers, **Plato** and **Virgil** spoke of Purgatory. *Plato* taught that souls who had lived a fairly good life, who had walked the middle road, were enclosed in a place where they were purified of their sins. *Virgil* maintained that souls couldn't free themselves of the sins they had committed while they were alive, and therefore had to go to a place where there was pain and where they suffered to atone for the sins of their past life.

††††

---

[13]1Cor 3:15 - 1 Pet 1:7
[14]Catechism of the Catholic Church #1023

What we have believed from the very beginning, right from the Old Testament till today, holds true for all time:

(1) Souls who are in Purgatory are those who have died in a state of Grace but have not been purged (cleansed), have not paid unresolved debts owed for offenses committed during the soul's time on earth.

(2) Purgatory is the place where Poor Souls are washed clean of all remaining blemishes, all imperfections, venial sins and faults. We say imperfections! When we think of God the Potter and the great care and hope He had for us at the moment of Creation, the image He saw of us, of what we could be, we then can look at ourselves and understand the imperfections the Church is speaking about, and the Divine Mercy of God to allow the slate of our soul to be wiped clean, while still on earth[15] or after death in Purgatory.

Purgatory and the New Testament

Jesus affirms Purgatory in Matthew's Gospel:[16]

"Whoever says anything against the Son of Man will be forgiven, but whoever says anything against the Holy Spirit will not be forgiven, either in this age or the one to come."

What is He saying here, you may ask, in reference to Purgatory? Jesus said that *"whoever blasphemes against the Holy Spirit will not be forgiven, either in this age or the world to come."* What did He mean by *"the one to come?"* He could not be referring to Heaven. Those who are already in Heaven have no need for forgiveness; their garments (souls) are spotless, made clean by the Blood of the Lamb. He cannot be speaking of Hell as that is irrevocable; the place from where no one returns. Those who are in Hell made the decision to sin against God and not seeking forgiveness, condemned themselves to this inferno of eternal damnation. Jesus had to be referring to Purgatory.

---

[15]Indulgences - see chapter on Penance
[16]Mt 12:32

Saints Augustine, Gregory the Great, and Bernard, to mention a few, teach that Jesus is plainly *"declaring that there is a place between Heaven and Hell where certain sins can be forgiven, in the world, beyond."* - Purgatory.

"Whether Jesus is referring to the obstinacy of the Jews or other unbelievers, in refusing to acknowledge the Truth, when He said: 'whosoever shall speak a word against the Holy Spirit,' one thing rings out clear and indisputable, Jesus is declaring that there is a place between Heaven and Hell where certain sins can be forgiven, in the world, beyond."

We hear Jesus speaking out about *"getting angry,"* that he who does so will be liable to judgment. He warns:

"Lose no time; settle with your opponent while on your way to court with him. Otherwise your opponent may hand you over to the judge, who will hand you over to the guard, who will throw you into prison. I warn you, you will not be released until you have paid the last penny."[17]

Again, is He not referring here to Purgatory? Is Jesus not saying, make retribution here on earth rather than suffer the pains of Purgatory from which you will not be released until the debt is fully paid?

Early Church Fathers, such as Saint Ambrose, Saint Augustine, Saint Jerome and countless others have all *taught* that this passage from Holy Scripture refers to Purgatory, when Jesus speaks of the debt being *"fully paid."*

†††

Holy Mother Church, the Mystical Body of Christ consists of three Churches: *The Church Militant* - we the faithful who dwell on earth, *The Church Triumphant* - the elect who are in the presence of the Beatific Vision in Heaven, and *The Church Suffering* - those who are no less members of the Body but who are in Purgatory.

---

[17]Mt 5:25-26

Those souls who dwell in Purgatory are more privileged than those who dwell on earth, as they are assured of entering into the Kingdom of God. They play a compassionate role in God's Plan to save His children for Himself. For God has always loved us; and as He is unchanging, His Love is unchanging; and part of that unchanging Love is the gift of Purgatory.

The three Churches commune together, praying for one another. We call that the Communion of Saints. *The Church Triumphant* prays for *The Church Militant*, who in turn prays for *The Church Suffering*. We, the faithful who comprise *The Church Militant*, pray to the Saints in Heaven-*The Church Triumphant*, for their intercession; and they, in turn, plead with the Lord on *our* behalf. *The Church Suffering* cannot pray for themselves; therefore they cannot hope for the intercession of the Saints in Heaven without the faithful-*The Church Militant*, praying in their behalf. However, once *The Church Suffering* become *The Church Triumphant* after they have entered into the Kingdom, they in turn pray for *The Church Militant*, *that's us*, especially those who prayed to get them out of Purgatory.

When we enter into the doors of Purgatory, we have the assurance we will enter Heaven. Our salvation is assured. We are saved by the Blood of Jesus. But we have time to spend in Purgatory. Our first reaction should be, "*Thank You Jesus, I'm saved.*" Our next reaction might possibly be, "*But Lord, do I have a long time to spend in Purgatory?*"

Don't for a moment think that anyone *doesn't* need your prayers. That's why a Guardian Angel always comes to you and whispers a name in your ear. Those who died need Masses! When we die, if you're still on earth, be sure to pray for us. We need prayers, not only now, but when we're burning off all our past blemishes in Purgatory. Say a Mass of thanksgiving that we made it into Purgatory, and then many many Masses that we get out of Purgatory.

Salvation through the Cross

**The Cross - Millions of Crosses
have been left by the Faithful in
Lithuania at this site known as
the Hill of Crosses**

*"'If you're the Son of God, come down from that Cross.
Come down and we'll believe.'* Sure they'll believe; they'll
believe anything, just no Cross!"

The shrill, piercing cry of the aging Archbishop Fulton J.
Sheen ricocheted off the walls of the Church of St. Agnes, in
New York City, on Good Friday, April 8, 1977.

"They say No mortification, no self-denial." He continued,
"Many say *'I'll believe anything! I'll believe He's divine! I'll
believe in His Church; I'll believe in His pontiff, only no Cross!
no sacrifice!'* George Bernard Shaw said of the Cross; *"It's that
that bars the way.'"* Sure it bars the way. "It bars the way to
hell."

Why did the saintly Archbishop Sheen cry out in anguish over the lack of respect for the unparalleled sacrifice our Lord and Savior made for us, so that the gates of Heaven would open wide for us? Was it in honor of a courageous but historic act made a long time ago, which has no relevance in today's world and is to be relegated to the archives of an ancient and dying Church? Or is the Cross a very real, very ongoing part of the Salvation environment of a very alive, always timely Church?

One of the many theories regarding the world of God on the other side of the curtain, which separates Heaven and earth, is that God's world is not restricted by time and space. That is one of man's limitations. In God's world there is no past, present or future. Everything is ongoing, progressive, happening. Salvation is a continuing process; Salvation is through the Cross.

We believe, when Jesus suffered His Agony in the Garden of Gethsemane, it was not only for sins which had *been* committed, nor only for those *about to be* committed which would bring about His total Sacrifice on the Cross, but for sins which *would be* committed in the years, centuries and millenniums to come. We believe the excruciating weight of the Cross was not only from its *physical* substance, but also the *spiritual* weight of the sins of the world.

A woman came up to Penny at a Trade Show in Los Angeles some years ago and tried to rip her Crucifix off her neck, shouting, *"Take Jesus off the Cross. Haven't you Catholics kept Him on the Cross long enough? He died once for all."* Penny's answer was, *"This* (Corpus) *is to remind me that I put Jesus back on the Cross every time I sin."* They say that Catholics are good at suffering. This might be so, but I don't think that's *why* we believe in the Cross of Jesus. Because of the agony Our Lord suffered for our sins, we have the courage to endure pain for *our part* in the Crucifixion. Another aspect of God's world that plays an important part in Catholics' attitude towards the Cross is, although the Crucifixion took place almost two thousand years ago, we believe it's still happening every time we break relationship with Jesus and put another thorn in His Head, another nail in His Body, another lance in His Heart.

Jesus said *"If any man will come after Me, let him deny himself, and take up his cross and follow Me."*[1] He gave us the gift of suffering, *Redemptive Suffering.* We are allowed to take the trials and tribulations of our daily life, the *physical* and *spiritual* sufferings which we may not be able to change or avoid, and use them for God's glory, by offering it up for the *Poor Souls in Purgatory*, or for a particular person on earth who needs our prayers.

There is so much the Lord allows us to do with our crosses. The crosses we carry are *our* crosses. They were fitted for us; they don't belong to anyone else. Don't ask to change your cross. You won't want your neighbor's cross because your cross is your cross. This is why we have a problem with the culture of death, assisted suicide, euthanasia. We are robbed of the Lord's gift of Redemptive Suffering. We are denied that gift of the Cross.

History about Devotion to the Cross

The tradition in Jesus' times was that the Cross was shameful and despicable. But to St. Paul and the other Apostles, the Cross and the suffering on the Cross was an honor, a step towards our Salvation.

"The language of the Cross may be illogical to those who are not on the way to Salvation, but those of us who are on the way see it as God's power to save."[2]

"Let us not lose sight of Jesus, Who leads us in our Faith and brings it to perfection; for the sake of the joy which was still in the future, He endured the Cross, disregarding

---

[1] Mt 16:24
[2] 1Cor 1:18-19

*the shamefulness of it, and **from now on has taken His place at the right of God's throne.**"*[3]

Our Lord Jesus was not only willing, *He chose* to die on the Cross to redeem man from the very condemnation of the Law,[4] which considered Crucifixion a disgrace, and imposed obligations on the people, but could not save. Jesus took a symbol of disgrace and turned it into a sign of Salvation.

Triumph of the Cross

When compared with the rest of Jesus' Life, the Gospel writers didn't go deeply into the Crucifixion and Death of Our Lord Jesus. To our knowledge, two of the Gospel writers were not there when our Lord died on the Cross. Scripture tells us, St. Mark witnessed the Crucifixion: *"And a certain young man followed Him, having a linen cloth cast about his naked body; and they laid hold of him."*[5] And we know that St. John was there with Jesus' Mother.

Did the others *not* write more, because they had not witnessed the Crucifixion of our Lord *first-hand*? Or was the Cross the problem? Was the Crucifixion considered a Scandal or a Triumph? It was almost as if it were a part of the life and ministry of their Lord that they didn't want to remember. They did speak about His being mocked, tantalized, degraded as no other before Him. They did recall Jesus' suffering and Humanity as He cried out, *"My God, My God, why have you deserted me?"*

But it was only John, who had actually been there at the foot of the Cross and suffered with Jesus' Mother, who saw the Cross as a *Triumph* and he wrote about it in this way. John's Gospel, which was the last to be written, is also the only one which treats the Crucifixion of Our Lord Jesus as a

---

[3]Heb 12:2
[4]Pharisees
[5]Mk 14:51

Triumph. *The Scandal of the Cross became the Triumph of the Cross!*

John's Gospel is unique. He dwells on different details than the other Gospel writers. *He was an eye-witness.* Our belief has always been that John regarded the end of Jesus' physical existence on this earth as the Triumph of the Cross, rather than the Scandal of the Cross. While the others in retrospect, may have understood and accepted the necessity of Our dear Lord Jesus suffering as much as He did, and in the manner He did, only John actually put it down on paper. He methodically tracked the incidents in the Crucifixion and Death of Our Lord Jesus and how they fulfilled Scripture: from Pilate's labeling Jesus "*King of the Jews*" and not giving in to the chief priests and elders, insisting: "*What I have written, I have written,*" to the seamless tunic in which Jesus was wrapped, woven in one piece from top to bottom - a sign of royalty or priesthood. It is also believed John referred to *unity* in the tunic as the *unity* of the Church.

St. Luke does not mention Mother Mary at the foot of the Cross because, since Luke was not present at the Crucifixion, it is most likely Mother Mary told him what had come to pass and she would not have wanted to bring attention to herself at the foot of the Cross, at the cost of us taking our eyes away from Jesus. But John mentions Our Lady at the foot of the Cross because it was John who was there with her and it was important to him that the Faithful know the part our Mother played in our salvation.

Mary stood at the foot of the Cross; Mary Magdalen was prostrate. Mary knew she had to be strong for her Son and those who followed, and so she stood, her heart breaking, crying silent screams inside, uttering not a sound.

The Cross that unites us

Jesus turned the Scandal of the Cross into the Triumph of the Cross. Through Jesus the Cross became a means of reconciliation, of unity. We are one under the Cross of Jesus! Jesus used this horrible symbol as the instrument of liberation from slavery to this world. St. Paul brings this point home clearly, *"As for me, the only thing I can boast about is the Cross of our Lord Jesus Christ, through whom the world is crucified to me..."*[6]

As Catholics, we believe, *the Cross* made us heirs with Christ in the Kingdom of Heaven. Jesus through the Cross manifested the Unity for which He prayed at the Last Supper. If there is one thing that binds all Catholics together, it's the Cross. If there's one thing we can all share, it's the Cross. If there is one thing which tells the whole world who we are without question, it's the Cross. But it's more than a symbol of all that we believe in. *It's a way of life!* Jesus gives us consolation through the Cross:

> *"Then to all He said, 'If anyone wants to be a follower of Mine, let him renounce himself and take up his Cross every day and follow Me. For anyone who wants to save his life will lose it; but anyone who loses his life for My sake, that man will save it.'"*[7]

> *"Anyone who does not take his Cross and follow in My Footsteps is not worthy of Me."*[8]

The Sacrifice of the Mass-the ongoing Sacrifice of the Cross

The Mass is the memorial of the Lord's Passion and Resurrection. *The Sacrifice of the Mass is the ongoing Sacrifice of the Cross.*[9] At Mass, we are called to recall the price He paid for us at the Sacrifice of the Cross. If we take this time to stand beside His Mother at the foot of the Cross and share His pain, His rejection, His Passion, His Love, His unconditional obedience to the Father, it will give us the

---

[6] Gal 6:14
[7] Lk 9:23-24
[8] Mt 10:38-39
[9] Council of Trent

strength to follow Him, if need be, on our own Way of the Cross to Crucifixion and Resurrection.

The Mass is known as **The Holy Sacrifice of the Mass** because on this Altar, the final sacrifice, that of the spotless Lamb, Our Lord Jesus Christ is made present on this Altar of Sacrifice. This *"sacrifice of praise, spiritual sacrifice, pure and holy sacrifice"*[10] is used to describe the Sacrifice of the Mass because this Sacrifice *"surpasses and completes all the sacrifices of the Old Covenant."*[11]

When we receive *Holy Communion, the Sacrament of the Eucharist,* we *are united with Jesus Christ,* Who through this unity *with His Body, Blood, Soul and Divinity* forms us into one body. We will be in communion with the Saints and the Angels in Heaven who are partaking of the *bread of Angels, the bread from Heaven, the medicine of immortality,*[12] *viaticum."*[13,14]

The Holy Mass is called *Holy* because it calls us to holiness, to go forth because of the metanoia (conversion) that has taken place, to go forth and complete God's plan for us in our daily lives, to be one in Him through obedience to His Church. The Mass is called *Holy* because the Holy One Who comes to life, dies and is resurrected (sacramentally) during this ongoing Sacrifice of the Cross and Resurrection.

---

[10]Catechism of the Catholic Church

[11]Catechism of the Catholic Church

[12]St. Ignatius of Antioch - ref. Catechism of the Catholic Church

[13]*Viaticum* is the name of Holy Communion when it is given in a public place of private manner to someone in danger of death, during an illness, or to soldiers going into battle. It may be given without Communion fasting at that time and may be repeated as often as required. When the Sacrament of Anointing of the Sick is administered at the same time, Viaticum precedes it. ref. The Catholic Encyclopedia - Broderick

[14]Catechism of the Catholic Church

The Cross of Jesus is mentioned in Scripture *twenty-eight* times. We would like to end our chapter with two of those passages: by St. Peter and by St. Paul, which cover a broad spectrum of our belief in, and devotion to, the Cross. They personify who we are as Catholics. They are as follows:

St. Peter

"He was insulted and did not retaliate with insults; when He was tortured He made no threats but He put His trust in the righteous Judge. He was bearing our faults in His own Body on the Cross, so that we might die to our faults and live for holiness; through His wounds you have been healed. You had gone astray like sheep but now you have come back to the Shepherd and Guardian of your souls."[15]

St. Paul

"The message of the Cross is foolishness to those who are perishing, but to those of us who are being saved, it is the Power of God.[16]

"And so, while the Jews demand miracles and the Greeks look for wisdom, here are we preaching a crucified Christ; to the Jews an obstacle that they cannot get over, to the pagans, madness, but to those who have been called, whether they are Jews or Greeks, a Christ who is the power and the wisdom of God. For God's foolishness is wiser than human wisdom, and God's weakness is stronger than human strength."[17]

And that, my brothers and sisters, is why the Cross is such an integral part of our Salvation!

We adore You oh Christ,
and we bless You
because by Your Holy Cross,
You have redeemed the world.

---

[15] 1Pet 2:23-25

[16] 1Cor 1:18 - The heading for this section is "The Paradox of the Cross.

[17] 1Cor 1:22-25

Index